Impulse
Control Disorders

Psychological Disorders

Psychological
Disorders

Impulse
Control Disorders

Christine Adamec

Series Editor
Christine Collins, Ph.D.
Research Assistant Professor of Psychology
Vanderbilt University

Foreword by
Pat Levitt, Ph.D.
Director, Vanderbilt Kennedy Center
for Research on Human Development

CHELSEA HOUSE
P U B L I S H E R S
An imprint of Infobase Publishing

Impulse Control Disorders

Chelsea House
An imprint of Infobase Publishing
132 West 31st Street
New York NY 10001

Library of Congress Cataloging-in-Publication Data
Adamec, Christine A., 1949-
  Impulse control disorders / Christine Adamec ; foreword by Pat Levitt.
     p. cm. — (Psychological disorders)
  Includes bibliographical references and index.
  ISBN-13: 978-1-60413-047-8 (alk. paper)
  ISBN-10: 1-60413-047-4 (alk. paper)
  1. Compulsive behavior. I. Title.
  RC533.A274 2009
  616.85'84—dc22   2008031271

Text design by Keith Trego
Cover design by Keith Trego and Ben Peterson

Printed in the United States of America

Bang EJB 10 9 8 7 6 5 4 3 2 1

This book is printed on acid-free paper.

All links and Web addresses were checked and verified to be correct at the time of
publication. Because of the dynamic nature of the Web, some addresses and links
may have changed since publication and may no longer be valid.

Table of Contents

Foreword

Pat Levitt, Ph.D.
Vanderbilt Kennedy
Center for Research
on Human Development

Think of the most complicated aspect of our universe, and then multiply that by infinity! Even the most enthusiastic of mathematicians and physicists acknowledge that the brain is by far the most challenging entity to understand. By design, the human brain is made up of billions of cells called neurons, which use chemical neurotransmitters to communicate with each other through connections called synapses. Each brain cell has about 2,000 synapses. Connections between neurons are not formed in a random fashion, but rather are organized into a type of architecture that is far more complex than any of today's supercomputers. And, not only is the brain's connective architecture more complex than any computer; its connections are capable of *changing* to improve the way a circuit functions. For example, the way we learn new information involves changes in circuits that actually improve performance. Yet some change can also result in a disruption of connections, like changes that occur in disorders such as drug addiction, depression, schizophrenia, and epilepsy, or even changes that can increase a person's risk of suicide.

Genes and the environment are powerful forces in building the brain during development and ensuring normal brain functioning, but they can also be the root causes of psychological and neurological disorders when things go awry. The way in which brain architecture is built before birth and in childhood will determine how well the brain functions when we are adults, and even how susceptible we are to such diseases as depression, anxiety, or attention disorders, which can severely disturb brain function. In a sense, then, understanding how the brain is built can lead us to a clearer picture of the ways in which our brain works, how we can improve its functioning, and what we can do to repair it when diseases strike.

Brain architecture reflects the highly specialized jobs that are performed by human beings, such as seeing, hearing, feeling, smelling, and moving. Different brain areas are specialized to control specific functions. Each specialized area must communicate well with other areas for the brain to accomplish even more complex tasks, like controlling body physiology—our patterns of sleep, for example, or even our eating habits, both of which can become disrupted if brain development or function is disturbed in some way. The brain controls our feelings, fears, and emotions; our ability to learn and store new information; and how well we recall old information. The brain does all this, and more, by building, during development, the circuits that control these functions, much like a hard-wired computer. Even small abnormalities that occur during early brain development through gene mutations, viral infection, or fetal exposure to alcohol can increase the risk of developing a wide range of psychological disorders later in life.

Those who study the relationship between brain architecture and function, and the diseases that affect this bond, are neuroscientists. Those who study and treat the disorders that are caused by changes in brain architecture and chemistry are psychiatrists and psychologists. Over the last 50 years, we have learned quite a lot about how brain architecture and chemistry work and how genetics contributes to brain structure and function. Genes are very important in controlling the initial phases of building the brain. In fact, almost every gene in the human genome is needed to build the brain. This process of brain development actually starts prior to birth, with almost all the neurons we will ever have in our brain produced by mid-gestation. The assembly of the architecture, in the form of intricate circuits, begins by this time, and by birth we have the basic organization laid out. But the work is not yet complete because billions of connections form over a remarkably long period of time, extending through puberty. The brain of a child is being built and modified on a daily basis, even during sleep.

While there are thousands of chemical building blocks, such as proteins, lipids, and carbohydrates, that are used much like bricks and mortar to put the architecture together, the highly detailed connectivity that emerges during childhood depends greatly upon experiences and our environment. In building a house, we use specific blueprints to assemble the basic structures, like a foundation, walls, floors, and ceilings. The brain is assembled similarly. Plumbing and electricity, like the basic circuitry of the brain, are put in place early in the building process. But for all of this early work, there is another very important phase of development, which is termed experience-dependent development. During the first three years of life, our brains actually form far more connections than we will ever need, almost 40 percent more! Why would this occur? Well, in fact, the early circuits form in this way so that we can use experience to mold our brain architecture to best suit the functions that we are likely to need for the rest of our lives.

Experience is not just important for the circuits that control our senses. A young child who experiences toxic stress, like physical abuse, will have his or her brain architecture changed in regions that will result in poorer control of emotions and feelings as an adult. Experience is powerful. When we repeatedly practice on the piano or shoot a basketball hundreds of times daily, we are using experience to model our brain connections to function at their finest. Some will achieve better results than others, perhaps because the initial phases of circuit-building provided a better base, just like the architecture of houses may differ in terms of their functionality. We are working to understand the brain structure and function that result from the powerful combination of genes building the initial architecture and a child's experience adding the all-important detailed touches. We also know that, like an old home, the architecture can break down. The aging process can be particularly hard on the ability of brain circuits to function at their best because positive change comes less readily as we get older. Synapses may be lost and brain chemistry can change over time. The difficulties in understanding how architecture gets built are paralleled by the complexities of what happens to that architecture as we grow older. Dementia associated with brain deterioration as a complication of Alzheimer's disease and memory loss associated with aging or alcoholism are active avenues of research in the neuroscience community.

There is truth, both for development and in aging, in the old adage "use it or lose it." Neuroscientists are pursuing the idea that brain architecture and chemistry can be modified well beyond childhood. If we understand the mechanisms that make it easy for a young, healthy brain to learn or repair itself following an accident, perhaps we can use those same tools to optimize the functioning of aging brains. We already know many ways in which we can improve the functioning of the aging or injured brain. For example, for an individual who has suffered a stroke that has caused structural damage to brain architecture, physical exercise can be quite powerful in helping to reorganize circuits so that they function better, even in an elderly individual. And you know that when you exercise and sleep regularly, you just feel better. Your brain chemistry and architecture are functioning at their best. Another example of ways we can improve nervous system function are the drugs that are used to treat mental illnesses. These drugs are designed to change brain chemistry so that the neurotransmitters used for communication between brain cells can function more normally. These same types of drugs, however, when taken in excess or abused, can actually damage brain chemistry and change brain architecture so that it functions more poorly.

As you read the Psychological Disorders series, the images of altered brain organization and chemistry will come to mind in thinking about complex diseases such as schizophrenia or drug addiction. There is nothing more fascinating and important to understand for the well-being of humans. But also keep in mind that as neuroscientists, we are on a mission to comprehend human nature, the way we perceive the world, how we recognize color, why we smile when thinking about the Thanksgiving turkey, the emotion of experiencing our first kiss, or how we can remember the winner of the 1953 World Series. If you are interested in people, and the world in which we live, you are a neuroscientist, too.

Pat Levitt, Ph.D.
Director, Vanderbilt Kennedy Center
for Research on Human Development
Vanderbilt University
Nashville, Tennessee

Overview

Impulse control disorders include pathological gambling, pyromania, kleptomania, intermittent explosive disorder (IED), and **trichotillomania**. These are all serious psychiatric problems, whether diagnosed or not. (Often they are *not* diagnosed or treated.) Individuals with these disorders usually know their behavior is wrong or strange but seemingly cannot refrain from the behavior.

The common denominator among all impulse control disorders is that they involve repeated impulsive acts over which the individual feels that he or she has little or no control. These acts cause problems for the individual and considerable distress.

People with an impulse control disorder feel swept away by what seems like an overwhelming and irresistible desire to act—to pull out their hair (trichotillomania); to gamble recklessly (pathological gambling); to set fires (pyromania); or to steal unneeded items (kleptomania). In IED, the individual is frequently overcome by a blinding rage that is often accompanied by a torrent of verbal and sometimes physical abuse of others. All of these disorders are deeply troubling and psychologically disabling to those who suffer from them; however, treatment can usually help.

RISKS FOR IMPULSE CONTROL DISORDERS

The risk for developing an impulse control disorder varies considerably with the type of disorder. For example, in considering IED, the level of risk is associated with age. One major study found that the prevalence was 7.4 percent for those ages 18–29 in the United States, dropping to 5.7 percent for those ages 30–44; 4.9 percent for those ages 45–59; and 1.9 percent for those 60 and older.[1] E. F. Coccaro and colleagues estimated a projected lifetime prevalence of IED of 11.1 percent.[2]

It is often difficult to ascertain the prevalence of most other impulse control disorders, since those who have them usually actively seek to hide their behavior from others, because of their shame and their fear of detection. In the case of pathological gambling, however, some experts estimate that pathological gambling affects 1 percent to 3 percent of adults in the United States.[3] In general, the disorder usually begins in adolescence, when the prevalence is about 4 percent to 7 percent.[4]

In one study of 204 adult patients in a psychiatric facility, the researchers found that 7.8 percent suffered from kleptomania and 6.9 percent were pathological gamblers. Yet only three of these patients had been admitted for an impulse control disorder, including two who were admitted for pathological gambling and one who was admitted for intermittent explosive disorder. Thus, impulse control disorders often go undiagnosed, even in clinical populations.[5] Of course, individuals who are admitted to psychiatric facilities are severely ill, and more research is needed on the prevalence of impulse control disorders among the general public.

Some studies indicate that the majority of people with kleptomania are eventually identified,while a small percentage are never caught or, if they are caught, may not be charged with a crime.[6] Consequently, most of what is known about kleptomania comes from individuals with kleptomania in studies of people who are either seeking treatment and/or admit they have a problem.

The prevalence of trichotillomania (chronic and severe **hair-pulling**) can only be guessed at by most experts, but some university surveys have indicated that the problem is present among 3.4 percent of females and 1.5 percent of males, although less than 1 percent fulfills all the psychiatric criteria for this disorder.[7]

Most studies on pyromania have been performed on children and adolescents, and these studies have found a prevalence of 2.4 percent to 3.5 percent in this population.[8] Research, however, has also indicated that many people with pyromania set small fires in their own backyards or in vacant lots. By committing impulsive acts in private, in most cases posing no threat

Figure 1.1 A woman with trichotillomania pulls hair from her scalp. *Wedgworth/ Custom Medical Stock Photo*

to other individuals, they are not identified as a threat to public safety. They are only identified by their own admission of their acts. As a result, the true prevalence of pyromania is uncertain.

COMMON FEATURES OF IMPULSE CONTROL DISORDERS

In the *Clinical Manual of Impulse-Control Disorders* (American Psychiatric Publishing, 2006), authors Eric Hollander and Dan Stein explain the cognitive aspects of impulsivity in impulse control disorders. These authors say there are three major components involved in controlling impulsivity, and all are problematic for individuals with an impulse control disorder:

> The first is the *inability to delay gratification.* Individuals with disorders involving impulsivity make decisions with the goal of attaining an immediate reward, regardless of how small the reward or what the likely long-term negative consequences of the decision are. The second cognitive component is *distractibility,* or the inability to maintain sustained attention on a particular task. Finally, impulsivity is characterized cognitively by *disinhibition,* or the inability to restrain behavior in a manner that would be expected based on cultural norms and constraints.[9]

According to one article on the common features of impulse control disorders, these disorders are generally characterized by three primary criteria:

1. The failure to resist an impulse to perform some act that is harmful to the individual or others;
2. An increasing sense of arousal or tension prior to committing or engaging in the act;
3. An experience of either pleasure, gratification, or release of tension at the time of committing the act.[10]

Figure 1.2 Men have been found to be more likely to have intermittent explosive disorder than women. *Color Day Production/ Getty Images*

Note that in any discussion of impulse control disorders, it is important to check the author's definition of what types of psychiatric problems are considered to constitute an impulse control disorder. For example, in some major studies, researchers have categorized as impulse control disorders such disparate psychiatric diagnoses as **conduct disorder, oppositional defiant disorder**, compulsive shopping, binge eating, Internet addiction, sexual compulsions, self-injurious behavior, and attention-deficit/hyperactivity disorder (ADHD).

This book, however, follows the explicit definitions of impulse control disorders that are provided by the American Psychiatric Association in the *Diagnostic and Statistical Manual of Mental Disorders IV-TR (DSM)*. The *DSM* includes only kleptomania,

Table 1.1 Comparison of Impulse Control Disorders, Typical Symptoms, Gender, and Average or Primary Age of Onset

TYPE OF ICD	PRIMARY SYMPTOM	GENDER PRIMARILY AFFECTED	PRIMARY AGE OF ONSET
Intermittent explosive disorder	Periodic and extreme rage, far out of proportion to the perceived harm, expressed by aggressive behavior	Males	Adolescence to young adulthood
Kleptomania	Overwhelming impulse to steal unneeded items from family, friends, acquaintances and sometimes stores	Females	Late teens to early twenties
Pathological gambling	Constant betting	Males	Adolescence
Pyromania	Firesetting	Males	Adolescence to young adulthood
Trichotillomania	Hair pulling, sometimes eating the hair	Females	Young childhood to adolescence

intermittent explosive disorder, pyromania, compulsive gambling, and trichotillomania as impulse control disorders. As a result, these five disorders are also the impulse control disorders that are discussed in this book.

COMPARING ICDS

Table 1.1 provides a comparison of the primary symptoms of each impulse control disorder, as well as a comparison of the gender that is primarily affected by each disorder, and the common age of the onset of the problem. For example, with kleptomania, the primary symptom is an overwhelming impulse to steal unneeded items from others, sometimes for the purposes of hoarding, and other times with no clear intent or plan for the

Table 1.2: Diagnosis via the Diagnostic and Statistical Manual: Symptoms of Impulse Control

KLEPTO-MANIA	PATHOLOGICAL GAMBLING	PYROMANIA	TRICHOTILLO-MANIA	INTERMITTENT EXPLOSIVE DISORDER
The person steals objects that he or she does not need or wish to sell. Increasing tension occurs before stealing and tension relief comes immediately afterward. Some individuals experience pleasure when they steal. Stealing is not associated with anger and the person is not psychotic. Behavior is not better accounted for by another diagnosis.	Individual constantly thinks about gambling. Gambles with increasingly greater amounts of money to experience excitement. Has tried and failed to stop gambling or to gamble less. If the individual tries to cut back or stop gambling, he or she is irritable and/or restless. Gambles to escape problems or relieve a bad mood. After losing money, must gamble another day to "get even." Lies to family members about gambling.	Has purposely set fires more than once. Experiences tension before firesetting and relief or pleasure when fires are set. Fascinated by fires. Fires are not set for personal, social, or political reasons or due to anger or as a way to obtain money. Individual is not psychotic or delusional. Individual conceals his or her firesetting from others.	Individual has pulled out a noticeable amount of hair. She or he is tense before pulling hair or when trying to avoid pulling. Person feels relief or pleasure when they pull out hair. Disorder causes distress and impedes interactions with others at home and/or on the job. Behavior cannot be better accounted for by another diagnosis.	At least several aggressive incidents were committed that resulted in a serious assault or property damage. Aggressive behavior is out of proportion to any stressors. Aggressive behaviors cannot be better accounted for by other diagnosis.

Source: American Psychiatric Association. *Diagnostic and Statistical Manual of Mental Disorders, Fourth Edition, Text Revision. DSM-IV-TR.* Washington, D.C.: American Psychiatric Association, 2000.

stolen item. Females have a higher incidence of this disorder. The person with kleptomania suddenly wants an item and takes it. In general, the onset of kleptomania occurs in the late teens to the early twenties.

In contrast, pathological gambling is a disorder that is characterized by repeated and impulsive betting. It primarily occurs among males, and its onset generally occurs in adolescence or young adulthood.

Pathological Gambling

Mrs. Jones said that if the sophomore art class did not calm down, she was seriously considering canceling the field trip to the museum. Most of the students groaned or sighed, but Melissa, 16, decided to take some odds on whether Mrs. Jones would really cancel the trip, and she quickly obtained interest from several students who received the notes that she passed them during class.

Melissa was enthralled by gambling, and she would bet on almost anything. Her grades had plummeted lately because of too many late or unfinished homework assignments. The homework that she was supposed to do seemed so horribly dull and unimportant to her compared to the thrill of betting on, well, practically anything. Melissa often experienced a mini-rush just thinking about what she could bet on. Her mind-set could be summed up in one statement: So many possibilities to bet on, so little time to get it all done.

Melissa's behavior indicates that she is in the early stages of a pathological gambling problem, and unless she and the others who care about her begin to realize that she has a serious impulse control disorder that needs to be treated by a mental health professional, her problem will only become worse. Already, Melissa knows that she is in danger of failing the tenth grade, which would mortify her parents if they knew. (Melissa has previously intercepted several notes home to her parents about this issue, so they were still in the dark about her failing status.)

Yet even if others *do* recognize that Melissa has a major problem, the fact is that she herself must also acknowledge that she has a problem before she can begin the necessary serious work that's needed to resolve it.

Melissa's brother, Andy, 22, is also a heavy bettor, but he really takes it too far, and Melissa knows that she'll never end up like him. He has been beaten up for not paying off bets that he has lost, and he's in debt to just about everyone, including their parents. In fact, the family hadn't heard from Andy for a few weeks and they were starting to get worried. His cell phone was disconnected, and when Andy's parents had gone to his apartment, the landlord said he had evicted him for nonpayment of rent, and he didn't know where Andy went. None of Andy's friends knew either. Melissa's parents said that if they didn't hear from Andy within 24 hours, they were going to call the police and report him as a missing person.

Many people would assume that because Melissa's brother, Andy, has a serious known gambling problem, Melissa's gambling would be glaringly evident to her parents. Yet, they would be wrong for several reasons. First, so far, Melissa has successfully hidden her gambling problem from her parents with excuses. Next, they are not really paying attention to Melissa because they're so worried about Andy. Lastly, many times even when a problem seems clearly apparent to others outside the family, often family members initially deny its existence to themselves, because to acknowledge it would be far too painful.

For many adults, it's fun to buy a few lottery tickets or even go to Atlantic City, New Jersey, Las Vegas, Nevada, or other places, and let off some steam by gambling a little money and maybe winning a few bucks. For some adolescents, it's also exciting to bet a small amount on who's going to win the big football game or on other major events in their lives. For others,

Figure 2.1 Many people enjoy gambling on occasion, but the pathological gambler thinks about gambling constantly. *James Marshall/Corbis*

however, their lives are *ruled* by the need to gamble, and they gamble as often as possible—morning, noon, and night. It's like an addiction, and pathological gamblers feel their hearts beat faster when they think about gambling as well as when they are actually gambling, especially when the stakes and the potential payoff are high.

For the pathological gambler, however, although winning is great, it alone isn't an end in itself. Unlike others who win, the pathological gambler won't walk away from gambling even if the winnings are huge. Instead, he or she will go right back to gambling again, telling themselves that it's an investment, and their good luck is sure to hold. For the pathological gambler, no amount of winnings could stop them from continuing to gamble. The only exception is if they choose to stop gambling and get the help they need to refrain.

It is also true that losing really big does not stop the pathological gambler, who will spend every cent that he or she has, draw a second mortgage on his home, max out all the credit cards, embezzle money, or take other criminal actions in order to put his or her hands on the money that is needed to continue gambling.

As Melissa herself has experienced, thinking about gambling and gambling itself are a major rush, and pathological gamblers want to reexperience that euphoric feeling over and over. This is true even when there are severe consequences to their gambling, as her brother Andy has already experienced.

COMPULSIVE GAMBLERS: WHO ARE THEY?
Most pathological gamblers are males, although females are not immune to this form of impulse control disorder. Among adolescents, research indicates that boys have a four times greater risk for the development of pathological gambling than girls.[11]

In general, the gambling fixation first takes hold in some individuals during adolescence, although sometimes the onset may occur during young adulthood. Pathological gamblers may be of any age, however, and they could even be elderly people. Experts also report that inmates in prisons, those under psychiatric treatment, and young individuals in gangs all have a higher risk of becoming pathological gamblers than others.[12]

STUDIES ON PATHOLOGICAL GAMBLERS
In one study of 200 people seeking treatment for their pathological gambling, nearly half the subjects had sought treatment from Gamblers Anonymous, an organization that is similar to

Alcoholics Anonymous and that helps people to cope with their gambling problem. Most (74.9 percent) of the subjects were male, and their average age was 41.3 years.[13]

The majority (61.9 percent) were employed full time or part time. Most (84.9 percent) met the *DSM* criteria for pathological gambling. In this group, the subjects had an average of 7.2 years of pathological gambling. About a third (30.3 percent) had some college education. Among these subjects, the average lifetime financial loss was $90,000, which is a large sum to most people.

In another study that compared male and female pathological gamblers, Hermano Tavares and colleagues interviewed 70 male and 70 female gamblers with an average age of 42.6 years. About 35 percent of these gamblers had received treatment for pathological gambling. The researchers found that a significantly larger proportion of women than men favored gambling performed through the use of electronic bingo and video terminal lotteries. They also found that the female gamblers had a faster progression to pathological gambling than the males, especially when they did play electronic bingo or used video lottery terminals.[14]

The female pathological gamblers also had a higher risk for depression, while the males had a greater prevalence of alcohol dependence. In addition, the women had a higher rate of smoking (74 percent) than the men (63 percent).

In a study of more than 43,000 subjects nationwide in the United States, drawn from the National Epidemiologic Survey on Alcohol and Related Conditions (NESARC), researchers looked at the risks for the expression of violent behavior among people with a variety of psychiatric disorders. In this study, about 22,000 subjects had one or more psychiatric disorders. They found that pathological gambling was a significant risk factor for exhibiting violent behavior, as were substance-use disorders, major depressive disorder, **bipolar disorder** and other disorders.[15]

The subjects were categorized as violent if they reported exhibiting at least two of seven different types of violent behaviors, such as forcing someone to have sex with them; getting into many fights; getting into fights involving the exchanging of blows with another person such as a spouse or partner; using a weapon like a gun, knife or stick in a fight; hitting someone so badly that the other person was hurt or required medical attention; physically harming another person on purpose; and/or robbing or mugging another person.

Of those subjects who had become pathological gamblers before age 15, 7.25 percent were violent. Of those who became pathological gamblers at 15 or older, 28 percent were violent—thus, the risk for violence increased with a later onset of pathological gambling.

The Families of Pathological Gamblers

Pathological gamblers are not the only ones who suffer because of their actions. Instead, studies have shown that their families also suffer many serious negative consequences. There are high rates of divorce and separation, as well as of domestic violence and child abuse and neglect. For example, according to an analysis by Martha C. Shaw and colleagues published in 2007, the divorce rate among pathological gamblers was 53.5 percent, compared to a rate of 18.2 percent among nongamblers.[16] In addition, the family members of pathological gamblers are more likely to also gamble as well as to abuse alcohol and/or drugs. Psychiatric disorders are common among the family members of pathological gamblers, who have a high rate of depression and anxiety disorders.

IS THERE A BIOLOGICAL EXPLANATION FOR OUT-OF-CONTROL (IMPULSIVE) GAMBLING BEHAVIOR?

Certain areas of the brain, particularly the frontal lobe, are associated with impulsivity, and as a result, dysfunction of the frontal lobe may be linked to impulsive behaviors such as pathological gambling as well as other problems. History has shown that damage to the frontal lobe can cause radical and negative personality changes. One example is the remarkable story of Phineas Gage, who suffered a railroad accident in which an iron rod was driven through the frontal lobe of his brain in 1848. Gage's life was saved by a resourceful physician, but he experienced an extreme personality change subsequent to his injury, transforming him from a normally affable person to someone who was obnoxious, constantly swearing, and generally objectionable to everyone who met him. Gage died of complications of his injury 12 years later.[17]

Another theory is that pathological gambling is caused by a brain disorder or dysfunction. For example, in one 2007 study by Ari D. Kalechstein and colleagues of 10 pathological gamblers that also included 25 subjects who were addicted to methamphetamine and 19 control subjects, the researchers used timed specific tests used by neuropsychologists to identify the presence of frontal lobe dysfunction in the brain.[18]

The researchers found that the pathological gamblers performed much worse than the control subjects in the comparison group. In addition, the gamblers performed similarly to the methamphetamine addicts on several tests that measured frontal lobe impairment, and on one test, the gamblers performed *worse* than the meth addicts.

Concluded the researchers, "These findings demonstrate that the severity of frontal lobe dysfunction in pathological gamblers is similar to that observed in methamphetamine-dependent individuals on frequently used clinical measures."

The researchers recommended that further research should provide even more information on this troubling data. They also said, "It is possible that these [frontal lobe] deficits are responsible for persistent gambling through a failure to inhibit behaviors or perhaps through an inability to adapt to continual losing."

RULING OUT EPILEPSY OR HEAD TRAUMA

In their book *Treating Gambling Problems*, published in 2007, authors William G. McCown and William A. Howatt warn that pathological gamblers who have epilepsy or who have had a history of head trauma should be very carefully evaluated, because in some cases, the root cause of their problem could be a neurological issue rather than a psychiatric problem, thus significantly affecting the treatment that is needed.

Say these authors about head trauma and epilepsy, "Epilepsy needs to be ruled out for gamblers who report fugue-like states [a state of feeling as though one is not really present in the real world] or who have a history of head trauma or other significant injuries. For reasons that are not understood, seizures may be more common among pathological gamblers. The most famous example is the Russian author Dostoevsky. . . . A history of multiple head traumas, developmental problems such as attention-deficit/hyperactive disorder, neural pathologies due to substance abuse, and other neurological problems are commonly found in people with a history of chronic gambling. These deserve evaluation by a neurologist and are often treatable."[19]

EXCUSES GAMBLERS GIVE THEMSELVES AND OTHERS

If pressed, most compulsive gamblers can offer plenty of excuses for their gambling, and they often truly believe the statements are valid justifications or explanations indicating that they don't have a gambling problem. Here are some of the most common excuses.

1. I'm just having some fun, and there's no real down side to doing a little gambling.
2. I am good at gambling and can make some real money for myself and my family.
3. Everybody has a hobby. Gambling is *my* hobby.
4. You only live once and you might as well enjoy it! Gambling makes me happy.
5. I know that I'm getting really close to a major win. I just have to stay the course; I can't give up now.

Statement 1, that gambling is fun, may be valid for many people, who spend small amounts of time and money gambling. It's when gambling becomes a compulsive need that there's a problem.

Statement 2, that the person is good at gambling, may also be true; however, making money for the family is rarely a good excuse because pathological gamblers also incur significant losses, no matter how smart or "lucky" they are. As discussed elsewhere in this chapter, when gambling is pathological, families suffer intensely.

In Statement 3, it may be true that gambling is a hobby, unless the person feels compelled to gamble and gambling adversely affects him or her with regard to their families and their jobs.

Statement 4, that you only live once and may as well enjoy your life, is a reckless statement that some pathological gamblers make to justify their irrational behavior. People's spouses or partners and children only live once too, and would prefer to have an actively participating partner and parent.

With Statement 5, that if you only stay the course, you're going to win, is a common excuse of gamblers to justify continuing to gamble. Sure, your luck may change; however, it may not. Even when the gambler starts winning, as discussed elsewhere, he or she feels compelled to continue gambling. They can't take the money and walk away.

GAMBLING AND AGING

Is your grandmother or grandfather a pathological gambler? This is not a joke, because some older people really are addicted to gambling. Pathological gambling is a problem for about 1 percent of people older than 60, based on a study published by Pietrzak et al. in 2007. This study compared the percentage of psychiatric and medical disorders among nongamblers, recreational gamblers, and pathological gamblers. Recreational gamblers may gamble frequently but their gambling does not rise to the problem level of the pathological gambler.[20]

Table 2.1 Comparison of Percentages of Psychiatric and Medical Disorders among Older Adults Who Do Not Gamble, Gamble Recreationally, or Who Are Disordered (Pathological) Gamblers

	ALCOHOL USE DISORDER	USE OF NICOTINE	MOOD DISORDERS	ANXIETY DISORDERS
Nongamblers	12.8	8.0	11.0	11.6
Recreational gamblers	30.1	16.9	12.6	15.0
"Disordered" gamblers*	53.2	43.2	39.5	34.5

*   Includes problem gamblers and pathological gamblers.
Source: Adapted from Robert H. Pietrzak et al., "Gambling Level and Psychiatric and Medical Disorders in Older Adults: Results from the National Epidemiologic Survey on Alcohol and Related Conditions," *American Journal of Geriatric Psychiatry* 15/4 (2007): 301–313.

Figure 2.2 Approximately 1 percent of people over the age of 60 have a pathological gambling problem. *Richard Smith/Corbis*

For example, as seen in Table 2.1, 12.8 percent of the older nongamblers in the study had an alcohol use disorder (either alcohol abuse or alcoholism). More than twice that number (30.1 percent) of the recreational gamblers had an alcohol use disorder, and some 53.2 percent of "disordered" gamblers—problem gamblers and pathological gamblers—had an alcohol use disorder. (Problem gambling is to pathological gambling what alcohol abuse is to alcoholism. They're both bad but pathological gambling and alcoholism are the worst stages of each problem.)

As can be readily seen from the table, disordered gamblers also have a much higher rate of smoking (nicotine dependence) and of suffering from mood disorders and anxiety disorders than those who do not gamble. For example, 11 percent of the nongamblers in the study have a mood disorder (a problem such as depression or bipolar disorder), while 39.5 percent of the disordered gamblers have such a problem. The disordered gamblers were more anxious, too, and had nearly three times the rate of anxiety disorders as the nongamblers, and more than twice the rate of recreational gamblers.

Out-of-Control Rage: Intermittent Explosive Disorder

Jim, 17, was really mad and he wasn't going to take it anymore. He was furious that the new guy in town, Tom, 16, had insulted him by laughingly saying that Jim's piece of junk car wouldn't last the year the way he was driving it into the ground. As has happened so many times before to him in response to a mild-mannered jab (or sometimes to just the funny way he thinks that someone is looking at him), Jim lashed out in a fury. He suddenly punched a very surprised Tom hard in the face, sending him sprawling into the dirt. Tom's nose looked broken and bloody, and he was holding his hands to his face, but Jim figured, hey, he deserved it, and he walked away.

The next day Jim was hurt and confused when his peers told him that he was a real jerk, a psycho, and a bully for assaulting Tom for no reason, and that he should pick on someone his own size. (Jim was 6 foot 4 and very strong, while Tom was about 5 foot 10 and skinny.) Some of them told him that he needed to see a shrink or maybe he should just sign himself into the psychiatric hospital. Then they turned their backs on him and walked away.

Worse, Jim found out that Tom had told others in school that he was going to complain to the police and get Jim arrested. Jim went to Tom's house and tried to apologize for his previous behavior, but when Tom opened the door and saw Jim standing there, he paled and slammed the door. Jim could hear a lock click into place, and he figured he'd better get out of there fast.

Jim has intermittent explosive disorder. When he gets angry, his rage builds up fast and spews out like a sudden overflowing of lava from a volcano, often directly and violently affecting others around him. The anger burns out fairly quickly, and within about 30–45 minutes, for the person with intermittent explosive disorder (IED), the entire issue is over and forgotten. (Although it's not usually forgotten by others who were directly affected by the person's rage attack.) At the rate that Jim is going, he'll end up in jail or prison soon—unless he acknowledges that he has a serious anger problem, gets some help, and works hard on mastering his periodic and overwhelming rages.

Most, but not all, people with IED are male. Gina, 15, has an anger problem that is seriously out of control. For example, most recently, Charlie, a fellow student, lightly tapped her on the shoulder to let Gina know that she'd dropped some papers, and she suddenly whirled around and kneed him in the groin. In agony, Charlie lay on the ground as Gina continued to kick him hard as bystanders tried to pull her away. Gina was upset that she was sent to the principal's office, because after all, Charlie had *touched* her. Gina did not like other people to touch her.

Jim and Gina both need help right away, and the people in their daily lives also need for these two people to get help, because their anger problems are out of control and are a danger to those around them. Compare the anger of a normal person, which in most cases slowly and steadily rises, similar to when you start to drive your car and you slowly and steadily speed up. Then consider the person with IED, who goes from zero anger to severe anger, somewhat like starting the car and quickly flooring it. It's also true that most people don't experience *any* anger over the relatively minor issues that can flood people who have IED with an immediate and overpowering rage. So, not only do IED sufferers experience anger beyond what is normal for a particular situation, they also experience

Figure 3.1 People with intermittent explosive disorder are subject to periodic and extreme rage, far out of proportion to the perceived harm. *Jim Varney/Photo Researchers, Inc.*

extreme anger in situations that would not anger a person without IED.

The anger problem has serious consequences for those with IED as well as for others around them; for example, one manifestation is **road rage**. Most people have experienced at least an obscene gesture made at them by someone who is furious because he believes others are driving too slowly, cut him off, and so forth. Others have been beaten or even killed by a person with IED.

SIGNS OF IED

Several past instances of aggressive behavior that resulted in physical violence toward others and/or destruction of property are signs of a person with IED. In addition, the rage that is exhibited by the person with IED is out of proportion to whatever has triggered it. The trigger can be a minor slight or even an imagined insult; the person with IED may think that someone insulted him or her, even when no one else thinks anything of any consequence happened.

In general, the rage of the person with IED lasts less than a half hour and there are frequent outbursts on a regular basis. The person with IED understandably has trouble holding a job and may also get into trouble with the law.

A person suffering from IED may also have depression or another psychiatric problem, but the periodic and extreme rage isn't accounted for by any other psychiatric diagnosis, including such possible diagnoses as bipolar disorder (manic depression) or a psychotic disorder. (Read more about other disorders that may appear with IED and other impulse control disorders in Chapter 7.)

WHO HAS IED?

In general, males are significantly more aggressive and violent than females, so it is not surprising that more males than females are diagnosed with IED. IED, however, should also be considered among angry females who do not fit the criteria for other diagnoses, such as conduct disorder, oppositional defiant disorder, or psychotic disorders.

Ronald Kessler and his colleagues reported on the prevalence of IED in the *Archives of General Psychiatry* in 2006, based on the National Comorbidity Survey Replication study of more than 9,000 adults nationwide. These researchers found that the lifetime prevalence of IED for all ages was 6.3 percent. Many individuals with IED exhibited violence during their episodes, or they at least threatened violence.

The first presentation of an IED is often seen during adolescence, and the average age of the onset of IED in Kessler's subjects was 14 years. In considering gender and IED, the researchers found that 9.3 percent of males and 5.6 percent of females had a lifetime diagnosis of IED.[21] The greatest prevalence of IED (12.1 percent) was seen among young adult males ages 18 to 29, as well as among individuals with less than a high school education (9.4 percent).

ROAD RAGE AND IED

Most people have heard of road rage, but is it real? Does it have anything to do with intermittent explosive disorder? The answer to both questions is yes. A study of college students and their reported driving behavior indicates that road rage is surprisingly violent, and it is also associated with IED. In this study, reported in *Behaviour Research and Therapy* in 2005 by Loretta S. Malta, Edward B. Blanchard, and Brian M. Freidenberg, the researchers compared 44 aggressive drivers with 44 nonaggressive drivers on a variety of issues. They found that about 20 percent of the aggressive drivers met the criteria for IED, compared to 1 percent of the nonaggressive drivers.[22]

The researchers also found that 18 percent of the aggressive drivers had been involved in one or more episodes in which they had caused damage to the property of others, compared to about 5 percent of the nonaggressive drivers who behaved in this manner. In addition, about 16 percent of the aggressive drivers had engaged in past incidents of punching assaults against others, compared to 5 percent with similar behavior among the nonaggressive drivers.

Other aggressive behaviors that were more common among the aggressive drivers were forceful pushes of others, property damage due to throwing, property damage due to vandalism, and even one case of nonfatal choking. In addition, the

Figure 3.2 A study published in 2005 found that 20 percent of aggressive drivers met the criteria for IED. *John W. Banagan/Getty Images*

researchers also found that the aggressive drivers were significantly more likely to have a family history of conflict and problems with anger.

IMPLICATIONS OF THE DISORDER FOR THE PERSON WITH IED

People with IED often experience social disapproval and even shunning. Their impulsive behavior may also lead them to end up in jail or prison. They may be harmed or killed, from being attacked by others who respond and retaliate to their extreme verbal and physical assaults.

Without treatment, the prognosis for the person with IED is not a happy one. Yet many people with IED are *not* treated. Kessler and his colleagues found that less than a third of the subjects with IED had received any treatment for their extreme anger. In contrast, 60.3 percent of them had received treatment for other emotional or substance-abuse problems, rather than their chronic anger problem.[23]

POSSIBLE CAUSES OF IED

Research has indicated that IED may have a genetic component. Violent behavior in a person with IED is often related to violent behavior occurring in his or her parents or other close relatives. An analysis of existing research, discussed by Emil F. Coccaro and Melany Danehy in *Clinical Manual of Impulse-Control Disorders*, revealed that about one-third of the relatives of people diagnosed with IED also had IED. In contrast, among people without IED, about 8 percent of their relatives had IED.[24]

Of course, sometimes individuals mimic the behavior of their own parents and other close relatives, so the cause of IED may not be entirely genetic. As yet, no specific gene has been isolated that is specifically linked to IED.

Some researchers believe that neurochemicals (brain chemicals) play a major role in IED, specifically serotonin or dopamine. Others believe that there is an abnormality in the metabolism of testosterone that leads to IED or that there may be an impaired neural connection between parts of the brain, such as the cortex and the amygdala (a primitive part of the brain that, when stimulated, causes strong emotional responses), which can lead to irrational and violent behavior. The bottom line, however, is that the cause of IED is still largely a mystery to mental health professionals.

DOMESTIC VIOLENCE AND IED

In a research article published in 2006 in *Medical Hypotheses* by David T. George and colleagues, the researchers studied 71 perpetrators of domestic violence. They found that about 10 percent of the perpetrators met the full criteria for IED and that *all* of the perpetrators were close to meeting the criteria.[25]

The authors said that upon close reflection, "Most perpetrators reported that prior to the violence they experienced not only an escalating sense of racing thoughts, anxiety, and fear, but also autonomic arousal (e.g., palpitations, increased breathing, and nervousness), extraordinary energy and a compelling need to defend themselves."

These perpetrators also reported feeling energized as they smashed their fist through a wall or punched their significant other. Seeing the other person who was cowering in a corner, bleeding, or physically injured, however, signaled to the perpetrators that the perceived "threat" against them was over, and only then did their anger subside.

Perpetrators of domestic violence are usually remorseful later, and they swear to those whom they have harmed that it will never happen again. Without treatment, however, it nearly always *does* happen again, partly because of the ingrained hypersensitivity of the person with IED, who feels regularly threatened by many real or imagined slights. When those feelings happen, he or she becomes heedless of the consequences of their actions, and acts with rage and violence.

Compulsive Fire Starters: Pyromania

Andy first started setting fires when he was a teenager. They were just small brush fires that were usually easy to put out, but sometimes they got a little out of control so Andy called the fire department. At first, the firefighters thought Andy was a real hero, and they clapped him on the back, praising him highly. After the first few warnings about fires from Andy, however, the firefighters began to wonder if he was somehow involved in these fires. How did he know that these particular fires had started in so many different places, sometimes far from where he lived? It was all just too convenient.

The fire chief began asking Andy's parents pointed questions, and Andy became frightened. Paradoxically, however, he was also really excited, because the firefighters said the fires were started by someone with real talent, and Andy felt as though it was a kind of praise. Unfortunately, this view of the situation did not lead Andy to seeking treatment for his pyromania, and his firesetting continued until the day he was caught in the act of starting a fire. Andy was arrested for arson, a felony. The prosecutor said he was going to seek to try Andy as an adult in court, which could mean a possible prison term if he were convicted. Only then did Andy wonder whether maybe he really needed some psychological help.

Many small children and some adolescents and adults are mesmerized by fire. After all, fire is beautiful, and it also provides warmth and comfort. Yet fire can be extremely dangerous—

it's something that you're not supposed to get too close to, which adds to its appeal for some people. Individuals with pyromania, also known as *fire starters* or **firesetters,** are those who feel compelled to start fires, despite the personal and financial risks involved.

Andy is unusual in that there are indications that many people with pyromania are never caught. Many people with pyromania start small fires in their own yards or on vacant lots, and these fires are not massive conflagrations that inevitably

Figure 4.1 Most compulsive firesetters are adolescent or young adult males. *Tamara Gentuso/iStockphoto*

will attract major attention. The risk of detection, punishment, and even incarceration, however, is always a possibility with a person who has pyromania.

WHO ARE PYROMANIACS?

Most compulsive firesetters are adolescent or young adult males. If the individual is under age 18, he or she may be diagnosed with conduct disorder based on a history of setting fires, as well as being diagnosed with pyromania. People with pyromania do *not* set fires out of a desire for revenge, because of their anger toward others, because they wish to hurt people, or because they seek any financial gain from firesetting. (In contrast, most arsonists *do* have anger, revenge, or a profit motive as the primary reason for setting fires). Instead, the pyromaniac is fascinated by fires, and enjoys starting them and then watching them burn.

Studies vary in their assessment of how many people are pyromaniacs, and estimates range from about 3 percent to as high as 7 percent of the population.[26] Some pyromaniacs have been charged with arson, although most experts report that many of the fires set by pyromaniacs do not rise to the level of arson, which is a crime of maliciously setting fire to property or burning down property for the purpose of insurance fraud. Also, some research indicates that pyromaniacs may check before they set a fire to try to make sure no people or animals would be in danger from the fire.

In one study by Yi-Hua Chen, Amelia M. Arria, and James C. Anthony, reported in 2003, the researchers found a firesetting prevalence of 6.3 percent, based on 284 youths ages 12–17 who had self-reported setting fires, contrasted with 4,207 youths with no history of firesetting. The researchers also discovered that the percentage of firesetting was twice as high among boys—8.4 percent for boys compared with 4.2 percent among girls.[27]

In contrasting personal traits between firesetters and non-firesetters, the researchers found a significant association of both shyness and aggressiveness among the firesetters, as well as high levels of feelings of rejection by their peers; for example, youths who felt highly rejected were 14.5 times more likely to start fires than youths who reported experiencing low levels of peer rejection. Shyness was not associated with starting fires unless this trait was also present with aggressiveness. Also, the combination of aggressive behavior and peer rejection were present in many firesetters, even when the trait of shyness was absent.

Said the researchers of this study, "The strongest associations with being a firesetter involved the triple combination of moderate-to-high shyness, aggressiveness, and peer rejection."

In another study by Sherri MacKay and colleagues of 192 male juvenile firesetters, ages 6–17 years, reported in 2006, the majority (69.6 percent) of the pyromaniacs were found to be white, and most of them lived with their parents (69.8 percent). About 30 percent lived in a foster/group home, a residential facility, or in another form of housing. The researchers also found that a heightened fire interest was predictive for firesetting during the 18-month follow-up period of the study. In addition, the researchers also found a correlation between antisocial behavior and fire interest.[28]

In another small study published in 2007 by Jon E. Grant and Suck Won Kim, of 21 adolescents and adults (7 adolescents and 14 adults) who had all received a lifetime diagnosis of pyromania (11 males and 10 females), the researchers found that age 18 was the average age for the onset of pyromania.[29] Of the adult pyromaniacs, the majority (57.1 percent) were high school graduates and six of them (42.8 percent) had either some college education or had received college degrees. The number of subjects in this particular study is extremely small, so the conclusions that can be made are limited. From this and other studies, however, it seems clear that pyromaniacs are not generally unintelligent or uneducated people.

Of the adults in the study, only three (21.4 percent) were female, while all the adolescents were female. This may be an artifact of the very small number of subjects in the study. Although most of the subjects (72.6 percent) reported feeling pleasure with firesetting, the researchers also found that the majority (90.5 percent) said that they felt extreme distress *after* the fires were set.

Figure 4.2 Some pyromaniacs have been charged with arson, although most experts report that many of the fires set by pyromaniacs do not rise to the level of arson. *Jeff Nagy/iStockphoto*

WHAT CAUSES PYROMANIA?

Some studies have indicated that some firesetters have reportedly experienced a past history of child abuse and family conflict.[30] More recently, theories for the causes of pyromania have run a gamut of possible causes; for example, as mentioned, Sherri MacKay and colleagues have found a correlation between fire interest and antisocial behavior among firesetters.[31] See Table 4.1 for the most recent theories of causes of juvenile firesetting. For example, some accept the explanation of the "opportunity theory," which is that the child has easy and relatively unrestricted access to fire, which he can use as either an instrument or weapon.[32] In contrast, in the case of those who support a "learning theory" viewpoint, pyromania is believed to be based on criminal behavior that was learned from the individual's family, friends, and others who directly or indirectly encouraged him or her to use fire inappropriately.[33]

It may also be caused by interpersonal failures. Said Graham Glancy and colleagues, "Social learning models hold that juvenile firesetting is the manifestation of interpersonal failures that lead to the deviant expression of aggression and control." As a result, firesetting may be exhibited by those with poor social skills who attempt to model others who are aggressive.[34]

Also, those who advocate "expressive trauma theory" to explain pyromania believe that setting fires is an expression of the individual's frustration and rage, and that this behavior is usually based on past child abuse or other major problems that the person with pyromania has experienced.[35] For example, the child may set her bed on fire as a cry for help from the sexual abuse she is suffering at the hands of her mother's boyfriend.[36]

Those who support the "stress theory" think that setting fires alleviates tension in the individual, or, alternatively, that it provides some excitement to an otherwise dull life.[37]

Table 4.1 Theories of Firesetting Origins

THEORY	ETIOLOGICAL THEME
Opportunity theory	Firesetting is a product of the open and relatively unrestricted access to fire as an instrument and/or weapon.
Learning theory	Firesetting is a behavior learned through association with family, peers, and subcultural forces that wittingly or unwittingly abet inappropriate fire use.
Expressive trauma theory	Firesetting is a manifestation of pre-existing childhood trauma and is used to vent frustration with victimization or other life circumstances.
Stress theory	Firesetting is a behavior that releases accumulating stress or seeks stress or danger in an uneventful life. It is often closely related to vandalism, shoplifting, and graffiti among juveniles.
Power association theory	Firesetting is a means for juveniles who are otherwise disempowered to attain power over people and/or the environment.
Social acceptance theory	Firesetting is motivated by the desire to gain acceptance by a peer or a peer group.
Social reaction theory	Firesetting is behavior produced in large part by the firesetter's knowledge that it will produce a substantial reaction or response from the wider society, such as the arrival of police and fire departments.

Source: Adapted from Charles T. Putnam and John T. Kirkpatrick, "Juvenile Firesetting: A Research Overview," *Juvenile Justice Bulletin*, May 2005: 4.

Experts who support the "power association theory" think that juveniles who feel extremely powerless in their lives turn to firesetting as a means to prove that they can and do have some control over their lives. Adolescents cannot legally drink alcohol or smoke, but a pack of matches is easy for most juveniles to access.[38]

With regard to the "social acceptance theory," if others in their peer group are setting fires, then firesetting is an acceptable behavior to that group, and the firesetter mimics this behavior to be one of the gang.[39]

The "social reaction theory" postulates that firesetters know that the fire department and/or the police will come to a fire, and they eagerly seek that type of exciting reaction. So they start fires themselves (as with Andy at the start of this chapter).[40]

AGE CATEGORIES OF JUVENILE FIRESETTERS

According to the U.S. Fire Administration, children set fires for different reasons, depending on their age. For example, when children up to age 8 start fires, they are usually accidental fires or started out of curiosity. Children ages 8–12 are intentional firesetters who may be driven by psychological conflicts, although they may be merely curious. When adolescents ages 13–18 start fires, however, they may be crisis firesetters, or those with a long history of playing with fire and who have either psychosocial conflicts or who are behaving in an intentionally criminal manner. There is also a minority of adolescent firestarters, ages 15–18, who are severely disturbed and may have criminal backgrounds.[41]

SYMPTOMS THAT ACCOMPANY PYROMANIA

People who have pyromania report feeling an increased level of tension before setting a fire, and this tension is subsequently released and then relieved by the act of firesetting. A similar level of tension is reported in all types of impulse control disorders, in part because of the apparent impulsive and compulsive natures of these disorders. For example, the person with kleptomania often becomes increasingly excited and agitated prior to stealing an item, and stealing something relieves these feelings—although often the kleptomaniac is overwhelmed with guilt after stealing. Compulsive gamblers may become almost manic just before or as they make bets that are long shots that they are convinced will pay off big.

Chronic Hair Pulling: Trichotillomania

Lauren, age 17, always wears a wig when she goes to school, or anywhere outside the house. In fact, she often wears a wig inside the house too, in case someone shows up unexpectedly. She doesn't particularly like wigs—in fact, she hates them. They're hot and sometimes look weird.

Lauren doesn't have a contagious disease, nor is she undergoing chemotherapy for cancer as many people suspect. She has trichotillomania, an impulse control disorder that causes people to pull out their own hair, often until they are bald and even eyebrow-less. (Lauren pulls out her eyebrow hairs too, but she carefully pencils in new eyebrows every morning.)

The word *trichotillomania* comes from Latin and Greek—*trich* for "hair," *tillo* for "to pull," and *mania* for a compulsive kind of madness. *Hair pulling*, however, is the more common phrase to describe the behavior (since most people stumble badly over the word *trichotillomania*, pronounced *TRICK-o-till-o-mania*). People who pull their hair out often concentrate on very painstakingly removing, one by one, the hair on their head and on their eyebrows (and sometimes removing all their eyelashes as well). Sometimes, however, people with trichotillomania also pull out the hair on their arms and legs and even the hair at the site of their genital area. Male hair pullers may pull out their chest hair. Men with trichotillomania often let others assume that they have male pattern baldness. It's a lot easier that way.

Often people make a general statement that they're so frustrated that they feel like pulling their hair out. Few people actually do this. Unless they get treatment, however, people with trichotillomania will usually continue the hair pulling, sometimes with brief periods of remission. They simply cannot help themselves without the assistance of a mental health professional and a lot of hard work, as well as appropriate medications.

In most cases, hair pullers lead otherwise normal lives, but their disorder often causes hair pullers to feel depressed or anxious, and they have a high rate of clinical depression and anxiety.

Hair pulling may begin by accident, but then the individual finds that it seems to relieve anxiety or stress, although only temporarily. Unfortunately, trichotillomania also creates stress, because the hair puller feels extremely guilty about this behavior or thinks that he or she must be mentally unbalanced because of it. Greater anxiety and stress often leads the hair puller to a need for *more* hair pulling, in a vicious cycle.

Some experts believe that trichotillomania is associated with obsessive-compulsive disorder (OCD), a condition in which the individual is compelled to count things, constantly wash their hands, or perform other meaningless and ritualistic tasks. OCD is an anxiety disorder. The *Diagnostic and Statistical Manual of Mental Disorders*, a manual that is used by psychiatrists to diagnose psychiatric disorders, characterizes trichotillomania as an impulse control disorder rather than an anxiety disorder.[42]

PULLING ACTIVITIES AND SUBTYPES

The time that the individual spends on hair pulling can range from one to more than three hours each day, and the individual may use tweezers to be sure to get out the exact "right" hairs. (The ones that the person feels *must* be pulled out.) Sometimes the pulling becomes aggressive enough to cause injury, bleeding, and even eventual scarring. Hair pull-ers frequently report that they feel pleasure or relief with their hair pulling, and they often set aside a specific time and place to accomplish this plucking task, according to Giuseppe Hautmann, Jana Hercogova, and Torello Lotti in an article published in 2002.[43]

Hair pullers may also exhibit other behaviors that are related to the body, and according to Hautmann et al., these activities may include nail biting, skin picking, picking at acne, nose pick-ing, lip biting, and cheek chewing.

High-Risk Periods

Experts such as Giuseppe Hautmann and colleagues have noted that there are occasions of high-risk periods when hair pullers are most likely to pull out their hair, and such times may include when they are reading, watching television, talking on the tele-phone, lying in bed, driving, or writing. In addition, hair-pull-ing activity is apparently much more prevalent in the evening for the overwhelming majority of patients.

Possible Pulling Subtypes

Some experts believe that there are two different types of hair pulling. Focused pulling is one form, in which the hair pulling is used as a means to control an urge or a sensation. Nonfocused pulling is hair pulling that occurs without the person even thinking about it, and this behavior usually occurs during sed-entary activities. Focused pulling is believed to occur in about 15 percent to 34 percent of hair pullers according to Douglas W. Woods and colleagues in an article published in 2006, while automatic (nonfocused) pulling occurs in a broad range—5 percent to 47 percent—of pullers. In addition, some people with trichotillomania are believed to exhibit both types of hair pulling.[44]

EFFECTS OF TRICHOTILLOMANIA

Many hair pullers avoid physical examinations of all kinds for fear that their hair-pulling will be discovered. Females in particular are afraid to go to doctors or other professionals because they worry that the experts may notice their unusual hairless condition, and then ask questions about it.[45]

Limited Career and Physical Activities

People with trichotillomania are often extremely careful in their choice of jobs and social activities. Because of shame they feel about their hair pulling, they may be careful to select jobs in which it is unlikely their secret will ever be uncovered. They also limit their social activities for the same reasons.

Medical Effects

There are medical effects that stem from chronic hair pulling. People with trichotillomania may develop scalp infections if they dig too deeply when pulling out their hair. They may develop chronic painful symptoms that directly result from their hair pulling, such as carpal tunnel syndrome or back and neck pain.[46] Often doctors misdiagnose the patient's problem because it rarely occurs to them that the underlying cause is hair pulling.

WHO HAS CHRONIC PROBLEMS WITH HAIR PULLING?

Most people with trichotillomania are females by a ratio of about 3.5 to 1, although it's hard to know whether this ratio is valid since it's easier for men to hide hair pulling than women and also men are less likely to seek psychological assistance than women. Experts disagree on exactly how many people have trichotillomania, and in their literature overview for *Psychosomatic Medicine* in 1998, Colin Bouwer and Dan J. Stein reported that estimates of the prevalence of trichotillomania

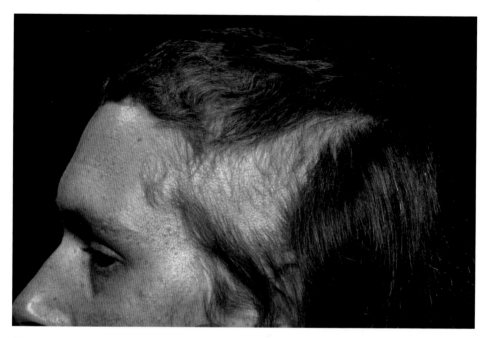

Figure 5.1 Hair loss resulting from trichotillomania. *NMSB/Wellcome Trust/ Custom Medical Stock Photo*

range from about 1 percent of adolescents and adults to 4 percent.[47] However, it can be hard to identify people with this disorder because most hair pullers do everything they can to hide their disorder, and unless they seek help, few people know about their condition.

Sometimes infants and small children pull out their hair; however, in general, if hair pulling occurs among young children, it is usually a temporary habit that disappears with time, much like the thumb sucking or rocking that infants and small children sometimes exhibit when they are tired or bored or when they feel stressed. In these cases, the behavior is more likely to be a short-term habit rather than an impulse control disorder, according to an article by Richard L. O'Sullivan and colleagues (1997).[48]

When trichotillomania has its onset later in life, however, such as after about age eight, it is usually associated with psychiatric problems.

In studies of children and adolescents with trichotillomania, reported by David Tolin and colleagues in a 2007 issue of *Cognitive Behavioral Therapy*, the researchers reported that most of the 46 child subjects spent about 30 to 60 minutes each day either pulling their hair out or thinking about pulling their hair out. Most of these children had significant bald spots, and they were also having major problems in school. In addition, the rate of problem issues within their families was high.[49]

THEORIES ABOUT WHY TRICHOTILLOMANIA DEVELOPS

There are many theories among mental health professionals as to why children or adults start and then continue hair-pulling. Some mental health professionals view hair-pulling as an addictive behavior or simply a means to alleviate tension, similar to several other impulse control disorders.

In one study described by Fred Penzel in his book *The Hair-Pulling Problem: A Complete Guide to Trichotillomania* (Oxford University Press, 2003), the addiction-blocking drug naltrexone was administered to patients with trichotillomania, and it resulted in a 50 percent reduction in hair-pulling behavior. This successful treatment was unfortunately not followed up, so it is not clear whether the treatment may be effective for the long term. In a more recent study reported in 2008, researchers found that 11 of 14 children (with an average age of 9 years) with trichotillomania responded positively to naltrexone.[50]

Behavioral analysts see hair pulling as a means to reduce tension, similar to firesetting in pyromaniacs or stealing in kleptomaniacs. According to Woods and colleagues in their 2006 journal article, one common trigger for hair pulling is a negative mood state, such as when the person is feeling angry, guilty, tired, indecisive, frustrated, or lonely.[51]

CONDITIONS RELATED TO HAIR PULLING

An estimated 5 percent to 18 percent of those with trichotillomania eat the hair that they pull out. **Trichophagia** is a term that refers to eating one's own hair, and the amassed human hairballs that subsequently develop are known as **trichobezoars**. According to Karriem Salaam and colleagues (2005), of those who eat their hair, about 37.5 percent are at risk of developing trichobezoars.[52] The masses of undigested hair remain in the digestive system, and eventually, after years of pulling out and then swallowing their hair, the hair interferes with the normal functioning of the digestive system, similar to a giant clog in a drain that will not let anything pass through. Surgery may be required to remove the mass.

Hairballs have been discovered after patients have seen their doctor about severe abdominal symptoms, such as vomiting, loss of appetite, and pain. The patient often denies having eaten her hair until confronted with the actual evidence. (Sometimes they still deny it.) Trichobezoars were discovered about a hundred years before trichotillomania was identified, according to Colin Bouwer and Dan J. Stein in a journal article published in 1998.[53]

Rapunzel syndrome is a phrase that is sometimes used for those who pull out and eat their hair, which becomes trapped in the gastrointestinal system. The most common symptoms of this syndrome are abdominal pain, nausea and vomiting, and gastric obstruction, according to Salleem Naik and colleagues (2007).[54]

Kleptomania: When Stealing Is an Unavoidable Urge

The silver bracelet was just lying there on the counter in the jewelry store, left there after a woman had examined it and decided not to buy it. The sales clerk was distracted, trying to convince the woman to buy something else, when Mona impulsively chose to take the bracelet. It wasn't at all her style, and she'd never wear it. She just had the urge to possess it—right now. Mona told herself that it wasn't really stealing because the people who owned this store were a bunch of stuck-up old rich people.

With her heart pounding, Mona rapidly pocketed the bracelet and casually walked out the door. Then she heard the store alarm ringing, and she knew that this time, she was really caught.

HISTORY

According to Jon E. Grant in *Clinical Manual of Impulse-Control Disorders* (2006), the first recorded case of kleptomania occurred in 1799, when Victorian author Jane Austen's aunt, Jane Leigh-Parrot, was arrested on suspicion of stealing some lace. This affluent woman faced several severe possible penalties, ranging from 14 years' imprisonment to being hanged; however, the jury found her not guilty.[55]

Kleptomania was first listed in the *Diagnostic and Statistical Manual of Mental Disorders-III* in 1980, and it was categorized as an impulse control disorder in the *DSM* in 1987. Some kleptomaniacs steal items that they hoard. They may be items that

Figure 6.1 Approximately 5 percent of all shoplifting is committed by individuals with kleptomania. *L. Steinmark/Custom Medical Stock Photo*

they could use, but instead they hide them and obtain pleasure from viewing them.

French physicians Jean-Etienne Esquirol and C.C. Marc were the experts who, in 1838, coined the term *kleptomanie* (in French) to describe shoplifting that was both irresistible and involuntary for some people.[56]

People with kleptomania may shoplift and, according to the *DSM*, about 5 percent of all shoplifting is committed by individuals with kleptomania.[57] Kleptomaniacs may also steal from their family, friends, and others.

WHO HAS KLEPTOMANIA?

Kleptomania is considered rare; however, when it occurs, it appears to transcend social classes. People who are wealthy and can afford to buy what they want are as likely to suffer from kleptomania as someone who cannot afford to buy the items they steal. Most people with kleptomania are females. In addition, many people with kleptomania are deeply ashamed of their stealing behavior; however, this does not stop them from repeating the impulsive act.

No one really knows how prevalent kleptomania is, since those who have the disorder actively work to keep their behavior secret, and may be successful at concealing the stealing from their own family and friends. As a result, the information that is available on people with kleptomania is primarily drawn from small case studies of people who have admitted that they have kleptomania. Based on these studies, it is known that thoughts of stealing often intrude on the patient's thoughts and make it hard for them to concentrate on other issues. It is also known that as many as half of people with kleptomania have other serious psychiatric problems, particularly other types of impulse control disorders, substance-use disorders, or mood disorders.

Most people with kleptomania actively seek to hide their behavior from others. They don't want to experience social disapproval and they don't want to go to jail. Nearly all of what is known about kleptomania comes from self-reports or studies.

In a 2003 study by Jon Grant and Suck Won Kim of 22 patients with kleptomania (14 women and 8 men, ranging in age from 13 to 68), the researchers found that age 16 was the average age of onset for the subjects and 73 percent of them had particular triggers for their urges to steal, such as stress, anxiety, loneliness, or boredom.[58] Some subjects, however, reported waking up in the morning with an overwhelming urge to steal something. Most (72.9 percent) said that the first time they stole something, it was from a store. Others stole from friends or relatives the first time that they stole an item.

According to research from this study, most stole household goods (59.1 percent), followed by groceries or food (45.5 percent), clothing (36.4 percent), tools or mechanical devices (31.8 percent), games/toys/sports equipment (22.7 percent), toiletries (18.2 percent), and books or music (4.5 percent). (Many people stole items from different categories of products.)

In order to resist the urge to steal, most of the subjects with kleptomania thought about the risk of getting caught (81.8 percent) and others stayed away from stores (63.6 percent). Some shopped with their family and friends in order to avoid stealing (31.8 percent), while others avoided leaving their houses altogether (22.7 percent).

Most of the subjects (63.6 percent) had been caught stealing in the past, and five of the subjects had been jailed for their crimes. The desire to steal was temporarily gone among those who were arrested, but within three or four days, those intense impulses were back.

The study also showed that stealing behavior often began during adolescence, but the average age when the actual symptoms of kleptomania began (such as feelings of pleasure or excitement at the time of stealing or an inability to resist the desire to steal) occurred about six years later.

According to Grant and Kim, "Why some subjects steal for years before it results in uncontrollable urges to steal and others develop a problem almost immediately is still unclear. A family history of psychiatric illness was the only predictor of developing kleptomania within 1 year of beginning to steal."

In another study by Elias Aboujaoude, Nona Gamel, and Lorrin M. Koran of 40 patients with kleptomania, published in 2004, the researchers found that most of the subjects were female (62.5 percent) and about half of the subjects were married (47.5 percent).[59] The average age of the onset of kleptomaniac symptoms was 17.1 years. Many subjects stole items frequently, such as four instances of stealing in the previous two weeks. The subjects were not poor: Their average annual income was $57,321. The overwhelming majority of the subjects (97.5 percent) lied to their family and friends about their behavior.

Only about 5 percent of the subjects said that they had ever received any medication treatment for their kleptomania, and they were given either sertraline (Zoloft) or fluoxetine (Prozac), both of which are usually prescribed to relieve symptoms of major depression, and which the subjects said helped very little. About a third of the subjects had received **psychotherapy**, which reportedly did not reduce their stealing behavior. (Read more about treatment for kleptomania and other impulse control disorders in Chapter 8.)

Another study by Franck J. Baylé and colleagues (2003) compared 11 patients with kleptomania to two groups: 29 patients without any impulse control disorders or substance-use disorders, and 60 individuals who had a problem with alcohol dependence.[60] The researchers found that the key feature of

Figure 6.2 A kleptomaniac acts on impulse, while a thief without kleptomania may have a plan. *Chuck Savage/Corbis*

kleptomania that made its subjects stand out from the other two groups was impulsivity. Using the Barratt Impulsiveness Scale, a questionnaire that determines the level of impulsivity, the researchers found that the total scores were significantly higher among the subjects with kleptomania compared to the group of psychiatric patients and the group of patients with alcohol abuse and dependence. For example, the total score of those with kleptomania was 72.1. This was a significantly higher score than among the comparison psychiatric patients (a total average of 57.3) or the subjects diagnosed with alcohol abuse or dependence (a total average score of 58.1).

THEORIES ON WHY KLEPTOMANIA DEVELOPS IN SOME INDIVIDUALS

Speculation on why kleptomania develops centers around biological theories and psychological theories.

Biological Theories

Some experts believe that brain chemicals known as neurotransmitters—particularly serotonin—could be implicated in kleptomania. Serotonin is a key neurochemical, and some research indicates that individuals with impulse control disorders are deficient in serotonin. Measurements have been taken of cerebrospinal fluid 5-hydroxyindoleacetic acid (CSF 5-HIAAA), a metabolite of serotonin function (serotonin levels can't be measured directly), and those individuals who are highly impulsive and sensation-seeking have had low levels of CSF 5-HIAAA, hence low serotonin levels. According to Grant, patients with kleptomania have high levels of impulsivity and risk-taking behaviors, and "diminished inhibitory mechanisms may underlie the risk-taking behavior of kleptomania." Thus, they may also be deficient in serotonin. [61]

Backing up this view, some studies have found that **selective serotonin reuptake inhibitor** (SSRI) antidepressant medications, including fluvoxamine (Luvox) and paroxetine (Paxil) have significantly improved the symptoms of kleptomania.[62] Other studies, however, have shown little or no improvement in symptoms during treatment with SSRIs. In one study, subjects with kleptomania were given escitalopram (Lexapro) or a placebo (sugar pill); there was no significant difference in their responses.[63] Intriguingly, in another study, three patients who were being treated for depression with SSRIs actually *developed* kleptomania, indicating that the increased levels of serotonin may have somehow triggered the kleptomaniac behavior.[64] (Although a sample of three people is insufficient to draw conclusions from.) It is hoped that future research will clarify this issue.

One reason why **antidepressants** or antianxiety medications may be partially successful with some people with impulse control disorders, including kleptomania, is that often these individuals are also suffering from depression and anxiety; it is common for those with impulse control disorders to have other psychiatric problems as well.[65]

Another neurochemical that may be associated with kleptomania is dopamine, which is also related to the opioid system (not to be confused with the drug opium), which affects cravings. Researcher Jon Grant says that evidence indicating that the opioid system is implicated lies in the fact that taking the medication naltrexone, which suppresses opioid receptors, is effective in reducing the urge to steal or commit other impulsive acts.[66]

Psychological Issues

Other experts have hypothesized that some psychological issues may lead to kleptomania. For example, the individual with kleptomania may have had an unhappy childhood full of turmoil. Marcus J. Goldman said that those with kleptomania had "unusually stressful childhoods (concentration camp survival, for example), marital turmoil, social isolation, and lack of self-esteem."[67] Goldman also proposed a typical woman with kleptomania as one who is age 35 and who began stealing when she was 20. "She may have a history of sexual dysfunction or sexual preoccupation and may be unhappily married to an emotionally unsupportive husband," says Goldman, who adds that she probably had a tumultuous childhood and may have been abused as a child.[68]

Some individuals with kleptomania say that they do not recall the act of stealing. Says Grant in the *Clinical Manual of Impulse-Control Disorders*, "patients reporting amnesia surrounding thefts often recall entering and leaving a store but have no memory of events in the store, including the theft."[69]

CONSEQUENCES OF KLEPTOMANIA

As with many other impulse control disorders, most people with kleptomania are deeply ashamed by their behavior and do their best to hide it from friends and family. Usually, however, they are eventually caught. With kleptomania, this can mean they are arrested and perhaps incarcerated as well, increasing their psychological distress. The person with kleptomania is humiliated and risks losing the respect of family and peers as well as his or her job and freedom. Yet the embarrassment and the risks that are associated with stealing are usually insufficient to stop the behavior. Additionally, many people with kleptomania are not treated because they refuse to acknowledge to themselves or others that they have a problem.

This refusal to acknowledge their problem, in addition to a basic denial of the problem, may partly be explained by the fact that kleptomania is different in many ways from stealing because you want something, as with those who shoplift because they can't afford to buy. For example, as described in

Table 6.1: Comparing the Kleptomaniac to Nonkleptomanic Thieves

PERSON WITH KLEPTOMANIA	THIEF WITHOUT KLEPTOMANIA
The kleptomaniac steals items he/she doesn't need and may not even like.	The thief often steals items that he/she wants to sell.
The person with kleptomania can usually afford to pay for stolen items.	The thief may be unable to afford the stolen items.
The tension prior to stealing is what drives the kleptomaniac.	The thief seeks items to use or illegally sell to others. The excitement (if it's there) is secondary.
The kleptomaniac acts on impulse.	The thief may have a plan.
The kleptomaniac steals alone.	The thief may have assistance from others.

Sources: American Psychiatric Association, *Diagnostic and Statistical Manual of Disorders.* Washington, D.C: American Psychiatric Association, 2000; Bernardo Dell'Osso et al., "Epidemiological and Clinical Updates on Impulse Control Disorders: A Critical Review," *European Archives of Psychiatry and Clinical Neuroscience* 256 (2006): 464–475; Grant, Jon E., "Understanding and Treating Kleptomania: New Models and New Treatments," *Israel Journal of Psychiatry* 43 (2), 2006:81–87.

Table 6.1, people with kleptomania usually steal items that they don't really need and sometimes that they don't even particularly want; it is thinking about stealing and then the *act* of stealing that provides the thrill rather than the item that is stolen. In contrast, the nonkleptomanic thief actively seeks items that they want themselves or they think may have good resale value, because the goal is to sell the items to others in exchange for some quick cash.

Psychiatric Problems Commonly Found with Impulse Control Disorders

Many people with impulse control disorders also suffer from depression and/or an anxiety disorder, as well as from substance-abuse issues, such as dependence on alcohol or drugs. They may also have other forms of impulse control disorders. Some individuals with impulse control disorders become so distressed by their problem that they have an increased risk for suicide, an issue that is also described in this chapter.

Mental health professionals use the word "comorbidities" to describe other problems that commonly occur along with the disease being actively treated. These additional psychiatric problems can make treatment much more difficult because different drugs may be needed and doctors must watch out for medication interactions—problems that occur when two or more drugs are used.

For example, in a study of pyromaniacs and their comorbidities published by Sherri MacKay and colleagues in 2006, the researchers found that two-thirds of pyromaniacs in the study had one or more other impulse control disorders, with the most common comorbid disorder being kleptomania. The majority of the subjects (61.9 percent) had an affective disorder (depression or bipolar disorder). In addition, one-third of the subjects had an anxiety disorder, and one-third had a substance-use disorder.[70]

DEPRESSION OR BIPOLAR DISORDER AND IMPULSE CONTROL DISORDERS

Many people who have an impulse control disorder suffer from depression. If depression is diagnosed in someone with an impulse control disorder, it is important that it also be recognized and treated.

According to Ronald C. Kessler and colleagues in their journal article published in 2006, about 37 percent of those with intermittent explosive disorder have a major depressive disorder, and about 10 percent have dysthymia, which is a low-level form of depression.[71]

Figure 7.1 In one study of pathological gamblers, 80 percent of the women were found to have a depressive disorder. *Ken Seet/Corbis*

In a study by Tavares et al. that was published in 2003, of 70 men and 70 women who were pathological gamblers, the researchers found the majority of gamblers were depressed, and the rate of depressive disorders was 80 percent among women and 63 percent among men.[72]

Other researchers have found significant comorbidities with kleptomania. In a study by Elias Aboujaoude, Nona Gamel, and Lorrin Koran published in 2004, of 40 subjects with kleptomania, the researchers found that major depressive disorder represented the largest percentage of comorbidities, or 35 percent.[73]

ANXIETY DISORDERS AND ICDS

Anxiety is also common among individuals with impulse control disorders. They may worry about why they are acting this way (pulling out their hair, stealing things, exploding over nothing) and they may legitimately fear the consequences of their actions, particularly if they are engaging in criminal acts. The fear and anxiety that the person with an ICD experiences, however, is usually subsequent to the act; for example, the individual feels compelled to gamble, pull out their hair, steal things, and so forth, and rarely worries about the consequences until *after* the impulsive act occurs. Then they may feel embarrassed, angry, and fearful.

Anxiety disorders are common in those with IED, and according to Kessler and colleagues, 58 percent of patients suffering from IED have one or more forms of anxiety disorder. The most common form is social phobia, present in about 28 percent, followed by specific phobia (24 percent) and then generalized anxiety disorder (about 19 percent).[74]

In a study of 46 children and adolescents diagnosed with trichotillomania, reported by David Tolin and colleagues, the researchers found a variety of comorbid disorders among these subjects; for example, about 13 percent of the sample had generalized anxiety disorder and 30 percent had some form of anxiety disorder. They also found that about 9 percent of the child and adolescent subjects had attention-deficit/hyperactivity disorder (ADHD). In addition, about 9 percent had major depressive disorder. Further, about 7 percent of the subjects met the criteria for obsessive-compulsive disorder (OCD).[75]

In a 2003 study by Hermano Tavares and colleagues that compared male and female pathological gamblers, the female gamblers had a higher rate of specific phobias (37 percent) than the male gamblers (30 percent). Their rates for OCD and panic disorder were identical or similar for the men and women; for example, 14 percent of the women had OCD, compared with 14 percent of the men. In addition, 11 percent of the women had panic disorder, compared with 9 percent of the men.[76]

SUBSTANCE ABUSE

Many people with impulse control disorders abuse alcohol and/or legal or illegal drugs. Abuse of drugs or alcohol usually makes treating the impulse control disorder more difficult. The person with an impulse control disorder is often trying to blot out their emotional pain associated with related depression or anxiety.

In a study published in 1999 that looked at 79 patients who were alcoholic and were hospitalized for detoxification, researchers Michel Lejoyeux and colleagues found that more than a third (38 percent) of the subjects also met the criteria for an impulse control disorder. The most common disorder that was identified was intermittent explosive disorder, with 24 percent of the subjects meeting its criteria.[77]

In addition, about 9 percent met the criteria for pathological gambling and about 4 percent met the criteria for kleptomania. Only 1 percent met the criteria for trichotillomania. (The incidence of pyromania was not studied.) The researchers found that pathological gambling was associated with a younger age at the onset of alcoholism, as well as a greater number of detoxifications.

Pathological Gamblers and Substance Abuse
Among pathological gamblers, alcohol is a commonly abused substance. In one study of pathological gamblers who were seeking treatment for their gambling, 64 percent of the males and 60 percent of the females reported using alcohol in the 30 days before treatment. Their levels of drinking were slightly down during the follow-up period after the study, but were

Figure 7.2 Among pathological gamblers, alcohol is a commonly abused substance. *Rainer Holz/zefa/Corbis*

still high among the men: 60 percent for males and 24 percent for females. Some of the gamblers also admittedly abused
marijuana before treatment, including 9 percent of males and
8 percent of females; however, during follow-up, marijuana use
was significantly decreased, to 1 percent for males and 4 percent
for females.[78]

In a study by Angela Ibáñez and colleagues published in
2003 that compared male and female pathological gamblers,
the researchers found that men had higher rates of alcohol
abuse/dependence than the women. For example, 15 men had
a problem with alcohol abuse/dependence (about 32 percent),
compared to only one woman (4.5 percent).[79]

In another study by Tavares and colleagues of male and
female pathological gamblers, the researchers found that there
was a significantly higher rate of alcohol-use disorder among
the men (27 percent) than among the women (6 percent).[80]

Intermittent Explosive Disorder and Substance Abuse

In looking at the prevalence of substance-abuse problems
among individuals with intermittent explosive disorder,
Kessler and colleagues found a higher incidence of substance
abuse than others; for example, 35.1 percent of subjects with
IED had a substance-abuse disorder. The highest percentage was among those who abused alcohol (32.9 percent),
followed by those who abused drugs (21.8 percent). Rates
of substance dependence (addiction) were also high, and 17
percent met the criteria for alcohol dependence (alcoholism)
and 10.5 percent of the subjects met the criteria for drug
dependence.[81]

Kleptomania and Substance Abuse

In a study by Aboujaoude, Gamel and Koran of 40 patients
with kleptomania, the researchers found that three patients

(7.5 percent) had a problem with alcohol abuse and two patients (5 percent) were diagnosed with cannabis (marijuana) abuse.[82]

DISRUPTIVE-BEHAVIOR DISORDERS

Many people with intermittent explosive disorder also have either conduct disorder (CD) or oppositional defiant disorder (ODD). According to Kessler and colleagues, among those with IED, about 25 percent of the subject also had ODD and 24 percent had CD.[83]

Oppositional defiant disorder is a childhood pattern of deliberate disobedience and constant challenging of the authority of adults. When present, ODD is usually exhibited by children by age eight. ODD is more common among boys than girls. Children with ODD frequently get into trouble at school, and they have a pattern of blaming everyone else for their own mistakes. They have few or no friends and are resentful and angry of others. They may act vindictively toward others.

According to the *Diagnostic and Statistical Manual of Mental Disorders (DSM-IV-TR)*, published by the American Psychiatric Association, "The essential feature of Oppositional Defiant Disorder is a recurrent pattern of negativistic, defiant, disobedient, and hostile behavior toward authority figures that persists for at least 6 months."[84]

Children with ODD are at risk for developing the more serious condition of conduct disorder during adolescence and adulthood. Individual psychotherapy is considered the best treatment for ODD, and parents must also become actively involved in learning to set clear limits.[85]

Conduct disorder, another disruptive-behavior disorder, may develop in childhood or adolescence. Symptoms include aggressive or cruel behavior towards animals and people, school truancy, running away, use of alcohol or drugs, the destruction of the property of others, stealing from others, and antisocial behaviors, such as bullying. Conduct disorder is more common among boys than girls. It is associated with genetic defects, child abuse, family conflicts and parental substance abuse.[86]

According to the *DSM-IV-TR*, "The essential feature of Conduct Disorder is a repetitive and persistent pattern of behavior in which the basic rights of others or major age-appropriate societal norms or rules are violated."[87]

According to the National Institute of Mental Health, some research has shown that the cold and unfeeling characteristics of children with severe conduct disorder or ODD may stem from insufficient brain activity in the amygdala, a part of the brain that responds to distress from others. The researchers found that children with disruptive-behavior disorders who looked at fearful faces had lower levels of amygdala activity than other children. Thus, disruptive behavior disorders may have a biological basis, although further study is needed.[88]

SUICIDE

People with impulse control disorders have an increased risk for suicide. A combination of the impulse control disorder, depression, and/or an anxiety disorder further increases the risk of suicide. Identifying the impulse control disorder and any comorbid conditions can help medical professionals better assess a patient's risk of suicide and prescribe the best combination of therapy and medications.

In a study by Otto Kausch that was published in 2003 on 114 military veterans who were also pathological gamblers, it was found that 45 subjects (39.5 percent) had made at least one suicide attempt at some time in their lives, usually with a drug overdose, and it was also discovered that 64 percent of those who had attempted suicide said that their attempts to end their lives were related to their gambling.[89]

Of the suicide attempters, most of them were white males. Somewhat surprisingly, the majority of those who attempted suicide were well-educated—50 percent had some college education, 9.1 percent were college graduates and 6.8 percent had advanced degrees. Less surprisingly, many had a problem with alcohol dependence (44.4 percent) or drug dependence (also 44.4 percent), and 26.7 percent of the subjects had a history of both alcohol and drug dependence.

The suicide attempters had high rates of other psychiatric disorders; for example, 52.3 percent of them had a depressive disorder (compared to 36.2 percent of the nonattempters), and 11.4 percent of these subjects had bipolar disorder (compared to only 4.4 percent of the nonattempters).

Said Kausch, "Pathological gamblers have high rates of attempted suicide. They are highly impulsive and suffer from high rates of comorbid psychiatric conditions as well as social disruptions. A combination of these risk factors very likely contributes to their potential for suicidal behavior."

Among pathological gamblers, a study by Ibáñez and colleagues that compared males and females found that pathological gambling had led to ideas of suicide in about 28 percent of the men and 23 percent of the women. About 9 percent of the women (and none of the men) had made a suicide attempt.[90]

Treatment of Impulse Control Disorders

Individuals with impulse control disorders urgently need treatment. In some cases, as with intermittent explosive disorder (IED), pyromania, and kleptomania, the individual is at risk for being incarcerated because of his or her behavior, as when the person with IED physically assaults another person, the pyromaniac is observed setting a fire, and the kleptomaniac is caught in the act of stealing. In other cases, as with pathological gambling, the individual may resort to desperate or even criminal acts to obtain money to gamble, thus leading to trouble with the law.

With trichotillomania, however, the individual is primarily harming herself, and in the process is severely limiting her options for having a normal and happy life. It's not so much hair pulling itself that prevents a person from having a successful life or career, but rather that the hair puller is so worried about being found out that she (or, occasionally, he) rigidly limits her or his life options.

Yet all people with impulse control disorders can be treated. There's no magic pill that cures anyone with an impulse control disorder, but there are medications and therapies that can create a significant turnaround in the person's world. This chapter describes both psychological and medication treatments for each type of impulse control disorder.

PSYCHOTHERAPY AND IMPULSE CONTROL DISORDERS

There are several major types of psychotherapy that are used to treat impulse control disorders, depending on the type of disorder. **Cognitive-behavioral therapy (CBT)** can generally be used to treat any type of impulse control disorder. The therapist teaches patients to identify and challenge their irrational thoughts and replace them with more rational thoughts. For example, thoughts such as "I *must* do this" (steal this item, set a fire, pull out hair, etc.) may be replaced with "I don't have to do this."

Author and researcher Nancy Petry offers a cautionary note on the use of cognitive therapies in treating pathological gambling in her book on pathological gambling (2005), and she

Figure 8.1 Many patients with impulse control disorders may benefit from psychotherapy. *Peter Berndt, M.D., P.A./Custom Medical Stock Photo*

provides this caveat: "Although cognitive therapies have a theo-
retical background, and the initial results of these techniques
appear promising, cognitive treatments that focus on modify-
ing erroneous cognitions should investigate whether cognitions
actually change in response to therapy. Studies should also assess
whether such changes are unique to cognitive therapy, as they
may be influenced by any type of therapy or even by natural
reductions in gambling behaviors that may occur independently
of formal treatment."[91]

CONSIDERING THERAPY FOR DIFFERENT ICDS
Many patients with impulse control disorders may benefit from
psychotherapy; for example, among patients with IED studied
by Bernardo Dell'Osso and others and reported in 2006, various
forms of therapy—such as CBT, family therapy, group therapy
and social skills training—were shown to be effective.[92]

Therapy for Kleptomania
Patients with kleptomania may benefit from **imaginal desensitization**, a therapy in which the patient imagines stealing an
item yet while in a relaxed state. According to Jon Grant in his
chapter on kleptomania in *Clinical Manual of Impulse-Control
Disorders* (2006), the patient is then instructed to imagine the
same scene, but to perceive herself as *resisting* the impulse to
steal. This thought process reportedly has been successful in
treating some patients with kleptomania.[93]

Another form of therapy is covert desensitization, in which
the patient imagines himself or herself stealing as well as the
consequences of being caught. In one case, a man with kleptomania was told to go to stores and imagine that he was being
watched by the store manager. This therapy enabled the man to
cut back the incidences of stealing, although the desire to steal
remained.

Trichotillomania and therapy

Behavioral therapy has been found effective in treating some patients with trichotillomania. In a study by Agnes van Minnen and colleagues published in 2003 on research with 43 patients treated with fluoxetine (Prozac) or behavioral therapy, the fluoxetine was found to be ineffective, but behavioral therapy significantly reduced the severity of the subjects' symptoms; for example, their hair loss before and after treatment was documented with the use of before and after videotapes.[94]

Behavioral therapy was composed of six individual sessions lasting 45 minutes and given every other week. The subjects' awareness of their hair pulling was increased by having them put strong perfume on their fingers, place bandages on their fingers or wear noisy bracelets. In high-risk situations, the patients were instructed to wear gloves. Patients were also given tasks that they had to complete to help resist the urge to start hair pulling, such as calling a friend or going for a walk. If they did pull their hair, the patients were instructed to do something boring or tedious, such as cleaning the bathroom or jogging for 30 minutes.

Giuseppe Hautmann, Jana Hercogova, and Torello Lotti reported in 2002 that various coping strategies were effective in treating trichotillomania. For example, with awareness training, the therapist works to make the subject extremely aware of the hair-pulling behavior.[95] The authors advise, "Ask the patient to slowly bring his or her hand(s) to the pulling area and, while doing so, to become exquisitely aware of the sensations in every part of the arm, from the shoulders to the fingertips." The patient is advised to practice awareness training for 12 minutes twice a day and is told not to pull out any hair unless fully aware of the behavior.

Another form of therapy for trichotillomania is called competing response. Hautmann and his colleagues advise that the patient should clench her thumbs inside her fists whenever feeling the urge to pull hair. They say, "Explain that this precludes pulling and that the urge will usually pass within this time." They also advise substituting another form of tactile stimulation, such as stroking a soft makeup brush or holding a string of beads that could be fingered. Relaxation therapy may also be effective.

Another form of therapy recommended by these authors involves self-monitoring, in which the patient is told to collect every single hair that is pulled in a day, put the hairs in an envelope, count them, write down the number of hairs and the date they were pulled and bring the envelopes to their next therapy session. Hypnosis is another form of treatment that may be effective.

Cognitive-behavioral therapy has been demonstrated effective in treating pediatric hair pulling. In a study of 46 children and adolescents seeking treatment at two outpatient clinics, researchers David Tolin and colleagues reported in 2007 that individual CBT was effective in 77 percent of the children and was still working for 64 percent six months later during follow-up.[96]

Compulsive Gambling and Therapy/Self-Help

Many pathological gamblers can benefit from a variety of therapies, such as cognitive-behavioral therapy, systematic desensitization, behavior monitoring, social-skills training, and other forms of psychotherapy, according to Pallanti and colleagues in *Clinical Manual of Impulse-Control Disorders* (American Psychiatric Publishing, 2006).[97] In addition, individuals may also benefit from self-help groups such as Gamblers Anonymous. These groups can provide a place where others understand their behavior and their problems. They can also help pathological gamblers understand that it is important to avoid the people and places that they associate with gambling, such as bars, casinos, and so forth.

Intermittent Explosive Disorder and Therapy

Some individuals improve with anger management therapy, while others benefit from group cognitive-behavioral therapy, according to Coccaro and Danehy in *Clinical Manual of Impulse-Control Disorders* (American Psychiatric Publishing, 2006).[98]

Group therapy may combine relaxation training with cognitive-behavioral therapy, teaching individuals both to relax and to rethink how they view the actions of others. More research is needed, however, on what therapies work in helping patients with IED control their explosive anger.[99]

Pyromania and Therapy

Experts say that therapy for individuals with pyromania is problematic because often firesetters refuse to acknowledge their acts and they lack insight. In addition, they often have a problem with substance dependence, particularly alcoholism, further making therapy difficult. Some experts have used positive reinforcement and threats of punishment while others have created prevention programs, according to Michel Lejoyeux et al. in *Clinical Manual of Impulse-Control Disorders* (American Psychiatric Publishing, 2006).[100]

MEDICATIONS AND ICDS

In many cases, medications can help the person with an impulse control disorder, whether the medication is an antidepressant, an antianxiety drug, or another medication. It should be noted, however, that no medications have been specifically approved for any impulse control disorder by the Food and

Drug Administration[101]; as a result, all medications are used in an "off-label" manner.

Kleptomania and Medications

Some individuals with kleptomania have been successfully treated with naltrexone, according to a small study of 10 people with kleptomania reported by Grant and Kim, in 2002.[102] In an even smaller study of 2 patients with kleptomania, Dannon, Iancu, and Grunhaus reported success with treating the patients with naltrexone.[103] Naltrexone is a medication that is usually used to treat alcoholics. Apparently this medication may also reduce the thrill that is associated with stealing for those with kleptomania.

Antidepressants, particularly drugs in the category of SSRIs such as fluoxetine (Prozac), may also be effective at treating patients with kleptomania by increasing the serotonin levels in the bloodstream. In discussions of medications for kleptomania, however, Grant (2006)[104] and Grant and Odlaug (2008)[105] said that some studies have indicated that lithium or topiramate (Topamax) may be beneficial in treating people with kleptomania, although further research is needed.

Anti-anxiety drugs (benzodiazepines) such as clonazepam (Klonopin) and alprazolam (Xanax) are sometimes used to treat individuals with kleptomania.

Pathological Gambling and Medications

In the case of pathological gambling, antidepressants have been demonstrated to be effective in many patients, particularly fluvoxamine (Luvox) and paroxetine (Paxil, Paxil CR). Other antidepressants that may help include citalopram (Celexa), nefazodone (Serzone), and bupropion (Wellbutrin and Wellbutrin XL), according to Dell'Osso and others in their

2006 journal article.[106] It is important to make sure, however, that the patient who is a pathological gambler does not also have **comorbid** bipolar disorder, because taking antidepressants could then lead to an emergence or escalation of manic symptoms in these patients.

Some gamblers benefit from mood stabilizers such as lithium.[107] Naltrexone has also been shown to be effective in treating pathological gambling. Note that naltrexone may be harmful to the liver and that risk should be considered by physicians. According to authors McCown and Howatt in their book *Treating Gambling Problems* (2007), nalmefene (Revex)—a selective opioid receptor antagonist medication—is a medication that is being tested with pathological gamblers. It is said to inhibit brain endorphins and thus decrease the desire to gamble.[108] Endorphins are brain chemicals that

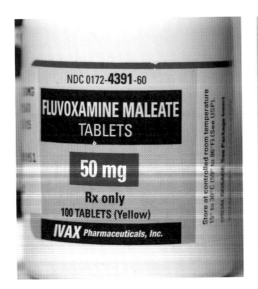 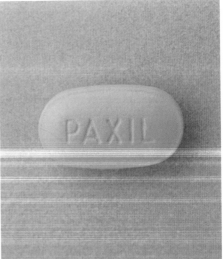

Figure 8.2 Antidepressants fluvoxamine (Luvox) and paroxetine (Paxil) have been demonstrated to be effective in treating many cases of pathological gambling. *Rosen/Custom Medical Stock Photo; Custom Medical Stock Photo*

cause feelings of pleasure, and if endorphins are blocked, then so is the pleasure. As a result, if naltrexone is effective, it is no longer fun to gamble, and hence easier to give it up.

Treating Trichotillomania with Medications

If the impulse control disorder is trichotillomania, clomipramine (Anafranil) has been demonstrated effective in several studies. Some child and adult patients with trichotillomania have been treated successfully with naltrexone.[109]

In some cases, a category of antidepressants that is called monoamine oxidase (MAO) inhibitors is used to treat impulse control disorders, particularly in the case of trichotillomania and kleptomania. MAO inhibitors block the action of the enzyme monoamine oxidase, which breaks down certain neurotransmitters, such as serotonin and norepinephrine, thereby increasing their levels in the brain. There can be serious side effects with the use of MAO inhibitors, however, so medications in other categories, such as SSRIs, are usually tried first.

Pyromania and Medications

With pyromania, Grant reported in 2006 that the antiseizure drug topiramate (Topamax, Epitomax, Topamac, and Topimax), combined with cognitive-behavioral therapy, eliminated the urge for starting fires in one person.[110] Of course, one subject is insufficient to generalize to all or most people with pyromania, and thus, further studies are needed—although it is difficult to find a large sample of individuals who are willing to admit to having pyromania. Other drugs used to treat pyromania include lithium and clonidine (Catapres).

Intermittent Explosive Disorder and Medications

Antidepressants, mood stabilizers (such as lithium and divalproex [Depakote]), beta blockers such as propranolol (Inderal,

Inderal LA) and pindolol (Visken), and even antipsychotic drugs have been used to treat people with intermittent explosive disorder, as well as antiseizure drugs such as phenytoin (Dilantin). Sometimes antipsychotics such as risperidone (Risperdol) are used to treat IED. There have been very few studies on individuals with IED, however, and these studies have found little or no improvement in the subjects using medications.

Other Medications

Another category of antidepressants that are sometimes tried with impulse control disorders are tricyclic antidepressants, which are older antidepressants such as impramine or desipramine, which contain three fused benzene rings. These drugs inhibit the uptake of serotonin and norepinephine at the nerve endings; however, they should be avoided in any patients with possible bipolar disorder or manic symptoms.

Yet another category of antidepressants that is sometimes used, particularly if the patient also has attention-deficit/hyperactivity disorder (ADHD), is a new category of antidepressant, the **serotonin norepinephrine reuptake inhibitor** (SNRI). This drug increases the level of both serotonin and norepinephrine in the brain, thus decreasing the risk for depressed feelings.[111] Examples of SNRIs are duloxetine (Cymbalta) and venlafaxine (Effexor, Effexor XR).

For more information on medications used to treat impulse control disorders, see Table 8.1.

LOOKING AHEAD TO THE FUTURE

Many clinical studies that are ongoing or have been recently completed as of this writing will hopefully lead to better treatment of impulse control disorders in the future.[112] For example, one new drug that is undergoing clinical trials for the treatment of trichotillomania is Nalmefene (n-acetylcystene), which would theoretically interfere with the production of glutamate, a neurotransmitter involved in the triggering of intense cravings. In addition, methylphenidate (Ritalin), a stimulant drug

Table 8.1: Medications Used to Treat Impulse Control Disorders

TYPE OF IMPULSE CONTROL DISORDER	MEDICATIONS OFTEN USED
Compulsive gambling	Antidepressants, such as fluvoxamine (Luvox), paroxetine (Paxil, Paxil CR), citalopram (Celexa), nefazodone (Serzone), and bupropion (Wellbutrin, Wellbutrin XL). Mood stabilizers such as lithium. Other drugs such as naltrexone or nalmefene (Revex) may be helpful.
Intermittent explosive disorder	Mood stabilizers such as lithium and divalproex (Depakote); antidepressants in the selective serotonin reuptake inhibitor (SSRI) class; beta blockers such as propranolol (Inderal, Inderal LA) and pindolol (Visken); antipsychotics such as risperidone (Risperdal) and antiseizure drugs such as phenytoin (Dilantin). Little success has been found with any medications.
Kleptomania	SSRIs such as fluoxetine (Prozac). Benzodiazepines such as clonazepam (Klonopin) and alprazolam (Xanax). Lithium has been used. Naltrexone works with some patients. Topiramate (Topamax, Epitomax, Topomac, and Topimax) helps some patients.
Pyromania	Lithium, clonidine (Catapres), topiramate (Topamax, Epitomax, Topamac, and Topimax)
Trichotillomania	Antianxiety drugs such as clomipramine (Anafranil). Some good results have been found with naltrexone. MAO inhibitors have been used but antidepressants in the SSRI class are favored because they have fewer side effects. Some patients have benefited from the use of topiramate (Topamax, Epitomax, Topamac, and Topimax).

that is used to treat children and adolescents with attention-deficit/hyperactivity disorder (ADHD), is being tested to determine whether it decreases symptoms of trichotillomania among children and adolescents who have both ADHD and trichotillomania. Zyprexa (olanzapine) is an antipsychotic medication and another drug that is being tested to determine whether it reduces the symptoms of trichotillomania.

Several drugs are being tested for their efficacy in treating intermittent explosive disorder (IED); for example, Prozac (fluoxetine), Depakote (divalproex) and a placebo are each being tested in one clinical trial comprised of three groups. With regard to kleptomania, naltrexone is being tested for its possible use in treating symptoms.

There are many medications that are being tested with patients who are pathological gamblers, including Nalmefene (n-aceytl cysteine), Campral (acamprosate), Namenda (memantine), naltrexone, Topamax (topiramate), Zoloft (sertraline) and Wellbutrin (bupropion).

Among patients with pyromania, naltrexone is being studied for its helpfulness in decreasing the symptoms of the disorder.

It should also be noted that patients with Parkinson's disease appear to have an increased risk for the development of some impulse control disorders, particularly intermittent explosive disorder and pathological gambling. Researchers are studying the effectiveness of Mirapex (pramipexole) and other medications in controlling these symptoms.

Finally, with most psychiatric disorders, situations of extreme stress tend to exacerbate symptoms, and patients with an impulse control disorder need to be aware of this risk.

NOTES

1. Ronald C. Kessler et al., "Lifetime Prevalence and Age-of-Onset Distributions of DSM-IV Disorders in the National Comorbidity Survey Replication," *Archives of General Psychiatry* 62 (June 2005): 593–602.
2. E.F. Coccaro et al., "Lifetime and 1–Month Prevalence Rates of Intermittent Explosive Disorder in a Community Sample." *Journal of Clinical Psychiatry* 65 (2004): 820–824.
3. Stefano Pallanti, Nicolo Baldini Rossi, and Eric Hollander, "Pathological Gambling," in *Clinical Manual of Impulse-Control Disorders,* eds. Eric Hollander, M.D., and Dan J. Stein, M.D. (Arlington, Va.: American Psychiatric Press, 2006), 251–289.
4. Jon E. Grant, et al., "Impulse Control Disorders in Adult Psychiatric Inpatients," *American Journal of Psychiatry* 162 (November 2004): 2184–2188. Available online at http://ajp.psychiatryonline.org/cgi/content/full/162/11/2184. Accessed January 19, 2008.
5. Ibid.
6. S.L. McElroy et al., "Kleptomania: A Report of 20 Cases," American Journal of Psychiatry 148 (1991): 652–657.
7. G.A. Christenson, R.I. Pyle, and J.E. Mitchell, "Estimated Lifetime Prevalence of Trichotillomania in College Students," *Journal of Clinical Psychiatry* 52 (1991): 415–417.
8. R.J. Kosky and S. Silburn, "Children who Light Fires: A Comparison between Firesetters and Non-Firesetters Referred to a Child Psychiatric Outpatient Service. *Australian and New Zealand Journal of Psychiatry* (1984): 251–255.
9. Eric Hollander, Bryann R. Baker, Jessica Kahn, and Dan J. Stein, "Conceptualizing and Assessing Impulse-Control Disorders," in *Clinical Manual of Impulse-Control Disorders,* eds. Eric Hollander and Dan J. Stein (Arlington, Va.: American Psychiatric Press, 2006), 1–18.
10. Bernardo Dell'Osso et al., "Epidemiological and Clinical Updates on Impulse Control Disorders: A Critical Review," *European Archives of Psychiatry and Clinical Neuroscience* 256 (2006): 464–475.
11. Howard J. Shaffer and David A. Korn, "Gambling and Related Mental Disorders: A Public Health Analysis," *Annual Review of Public Health* 23 (2002): 171–212.
12. H.J. Shaffer, M.N. Hall, and J. Vander Bilt, "Estimating the Prevalence of Disordered Gambling Behavior in the United States and Canada: A Research Synthesis," *American Journal of Public Health* 89/9 (1999): 1369–1376. Available online at http://www.ajph.org/cgi/content/abstract/89/9/1369?ck-nck. Accessed January 19, 2008.
13. Tony Toneatto, "Relationship Between Gender and Substance Use Among Treatment-seeking Gamblers." Gambling Research: The Electronic Journal of Gambling Issues. June 23, 2002. Available online at http://www.camh.net/egambling/issue1/research. Accessed April 23, 2008.

14. Hermano Tavares, et al., "Factors at Play in Faster Progression for Female Pathological Gamblers: An Exploratory Analysis," *Journal of Clinical Psychiatry* 65/4 (April 2003): 433–438.

15. Attila J. Pulay, et al., "Violent Behavior and DSM-IV Psychiatric Disorders: Results from the National Epidemiologic Survey on Alcohol and Related Conditions," *Journal of Clinical Psychiatry* 69 (1) (2008): 12-22 Abstract available online at http://www.psychiatrist.com/abstracts/abstracts.asp?abstract=200801/010801.htm. Accessed April 23, 2008.

16. Martha C. Shaw et al., "The Effect of Pathological Gambling on Families, Marriages, and Children," *CNS Spectrums* 12/8 (2007): 615–622. Available online at http://www.cnsspectrums.com/aspx/articledetail.aspx?articleid=1162 Accessed April 23, 2008.

17. Thomas, C. Neylan, "Frontal Lobe Function: Mr. Phineas Gage's Famous Injury," *Journal of Neuropsychiatry and Clinical Neuroscience* 11/1 (Spring 1999): 280–281; John M. Harlow, "Passage of an Iron Rod Through the Head," *Journal of Neuropsychiatry and Clinical Neuroscience* 11/1 (Spring 1999): 281–283.

18. Ari D. Kalechstein et al., "Pathological Gamblers Demonstrate Frontal Lobe Impairment Consistent with That of Methamphetamine-Dependent Individuals," *Journal of Neuropsychiatry and Clinical Neurosciences* 19 (2007): 298–303.

19. William G. McCown and William A. Howatt, *Treating Gambling Problems*. New York: John Wiley & Sons, 2007.

20. Robert H. Pietrzak et al., "Gambling Level and Psychiatric and Medical Disorders in Older Adults: Results from the National Epidemiologic Survey on Alcohol and Related Conditions," *American Journal of Geriatric Psychiatry* 15/4 (2007): 301–313.

21. Ronald C. Kessler et al., "The Prevalence and Correlates of DSM-IV Intermittent Explosive Disorder in the National Comorbidity Survey Replication," *Archives of General Psychiatry* 63 (June 2006): 669–678.

22. Loretta S. Malta, Edward B. Blanchard, and Brian M. Freidenberg, "Psychiatric and Behavioral Problems in Aggressive Drivers," *Behaviour Research and Therapy* 43 (2005): 1467–1484.

23. Kessler et al., "The Prevalence and Correlates of DSM-IV Intermittent Explosive Disorder in the National Comorbidity Survey Replication," 669–678.

24. Emil F. Coccaro and Melany Danehy, "Intermittent Explosive Disorder," in *Clinical Manual of Impulse-Control Disorders*, eds. Eric Hollander and Dan J. Stein (Arlington, Va.: American Psychiatric Press, 2006), 19–37.

25. David T. George et al., "A Model Linking Biology, Behavior and Psychiatric Diagnoses in Perpetrators of Domestic Violence," *Medical Hypotheses* 67 (2006): 345–353.

26. Jon E. Grant and Suck Won Kim, "Clinical Characteristics

and Psychiatric Comorbidity of Pyromania," *Journal of Clinical Psychiatry* 68/11 (November 2007): 1717–1722.

27. Yi-Hua Chen, Amelia M. Arria, and James C. Anthony, "Firesetting in Adolescence and Being Aggressive, Shy, and Rejected by Peers: New Epidemiologic Evidence from a National Sample Survey." *Journal of the American Academy of Psychiatry and the Law* 31 (2003): 44–52.

28. Sherri MacKay et al., "Fire Interest and Antisociality as Risk Factors in the Severity and Persistence of Juvenile Firesetting," *Journal of the American Academy of Child Adolescent Psychiatry* 546/9 (2006) 1077–1084.

29. Grant and Kim, "Clinical Characteristics and Psychiatric Comorbidity of Pyromania," 1717–1722.

30. L.F. Lowenstein, "The Etiology, Diagnosis, and Treatment of the Fire-setting Behaviour of Children," *Child Psychiatry and Human Development* 19/3 (March 1989): 186–194; David J. Kolko and Alan E. Kazdin, "The Emergence and Recurrence of Child Firesetting: A One-Year Prospective Study," *Journal of Abnormal Child Psychology* 20/1 (February 1992): 17–37.

31. MacKay et al., "Fire Interest and Antisociality," 1077–1084.

32. Lawrence E. Cohen and Marcus Felson, "Social Change and Crime Rate Trends: A Routine Activity Approach," *American Sociological Review* 44/4 (!979): 588–608.

33. D. Kolko and A. Kazdin, "A Conceptualization of Firesetting in Children and Adolescents," *Journal of Abnormal Child Psychology* 14 (1986): 49–61.

34. Graham Glancy et al., "Commentary: Models and Correlates of Firesetting Behavior," *Journal of the American Academy of Psychiatry Law* 31 (2003): 53–57.

35. Lowenstein, "The Etiology, Diagnosis and Treatment of the Fire-Setting Behaviour of Children," 186–194.

36. Charles T. Putnam and John T. Kirkpatrick, "Juvenile Firesetting: A Research Overview," *Juvenile Justice Bulletin*, May 2005: 1–8.

37. Stephen Lyng, "Edgework: A Social Psychological Analysis of Voluntary Risk Taking," *American Journal of Sociology* 95/4 (1990): 851–886.

38 G. Sakheim and E. Osborn, "A Psychological Profile of Juvenile Firesetters in Residential Treatment: A Replication Study." *Child Welfare* 65/5 (1986): 495–502.

39. Tracey Swaffer and Clive R. Hollin, "Adolescent Firesetting: Why Do They Say They Do It?" *Journal of Adolescence* 18 (1995): 619–623.

40. L. Macht and J. Mack, "The Firesetter Syndrome," *Psychiatry* 31 (1968): 277–288.

41. United States Fire Administration, "Children and Fire." *Topical Fire Research Series* 1/6 (2001). Available online at http://www.usfa.dhs.gov/downloads/pdf/tfrs/v1i6-508.pdf. Downloaded March 20, 2008.

42. American Psychiatric Association, *Diagnostic and Statistical Manual of Disorders. Fourth Edition, Text*

Revision. DSM-IV-TR. Washington, D.C: American Psychiatric Association, 2000. Washington, D.C.: American Psychiatric Association, 2000.

43. Giuseppe Hautmann, Jana Hercogova, and Torello Lotti, "Trichotillomania," *Journal of the American Academy of Dermatology* 46 (2002): 807–826.

44. Douglas W. Woods et al., "Understanding and Treating Trichotillomania: What We Know and What We Don't Know," *Psychiatric Clinics of North America* 29 (2006): 487–501.

45. Richard O'Sullivan et al., "Trichotillomania: Behavioral symptom or clinical syndrome?" *American Journal of Psychiatry* 154/10 (1997): 1442–1449.

46. R.L. O'Sullivan et al., "Trichotillomania and carpal tunnel syndrome," *Journal of Clinical Psychiatry* 57 (1996): 174; O'Sullivan et al., "Trichotillomania: Behavioral symptom or clinical syndrome?" 1442–1449.

47. Colin Bouwer and Dan J. Stein, "Trichobezoars in trichotillomania: Case report and literature review," *Psychosomatic Medicine* 60 (1998): 658–660.

48. O'Sullivan et al., "Trichotillomania: Behavioral symptom or clinical syndrome?" 1442–1449.

49. David Tolin et al., "Pediatric Trichotillomania: Descriptive Psychopathology and an Open Trial of Cognitive Behavioral Therapy," *Cognitive Behaviour Therapy* 36/3 (2007) :129–144.

50. Avinash De Sousa, "An Open-label Pilot Study of Naltrexone in Childhood-Onset Trichotillomania," *Journal of Child and Adolescent Psychopharmacology* 18/1 (2008): 30–33.

51. Woods et al., "Understanding and treating trichotillomania," 487–501.

52. Karriem Salaam, et al., "Untreated trichotillomania and trichophagia: Surgical emergency in a teenage girl," *Psychosomatics* 46/4 (July-August, 2005): 362–366.

53. Colin Bouwer and Dan J. Stein, "Trichobezoars in trichotillomania: Case report and literature review," *Psychosomatic Medicine* 60 (1998): 658–660.

54. Salleem Naik et al., "Rapunzel Syndrome Reviewed and Redefined," *Digestive Surgery* 24 (2007): 157–161.

55. Jon E. Grant, "Kleptomania," in *Clinical Manual of Impulse-Control Disorders,* eds. Eric Hollander, and Dan J. Stein (Washington, D.C.: American Psychiatric Publishing, 2006), 175–201.

56. Jon E. Grant, "Understanding and Treating Kleptomania: New Models and New Treatments," *Israel Journal of Psychiatry and Related Sciences* 43/2 (2006): 81–87.

57. American Psychiatric Association, *Diagnostic and Statistical Manual of Disorders IV-TR.* Washington, D.C: American Psychiatric Association, 2000.

58. Jon E. Grant and Suck Won Kim, "Clinical characteristics and associated psychopathology of 22 patients with kleptomania," *Comprehensive Psychiatry* 43/5 (2003): 378–384.

59. Elias Aboujaoude, Nona Gamel, and Lorrin M. Kora, "Overview of kleptomania and phenomenological description of 40 patients," *Primary Care Companion to the Journal of Clinical Psychiatry* 6/6 (2004): 244–247.

60. Franck J. Baylé, Hervé Caci, Bruno Millet, Sami Richa, and Jean-Pierre Olé, "Psychopathology and comorbidity of psychiatric disorders in patients with kleptomania," *American Journal of Psychiatry* 160/8 (2003): 1509–1513.

61. Jon Grant, "Kleptomania," in *Clinical Manual of Impulse-Control Disorders,* eds. Eric Hollander and Dan J. Stein (Arlington, Va.: American Psychiatric Press, 2006), 175–201.

62. R. Durst et al., "Kleptomania: Diagnosis and Treatment Options," CNS Drugs 15/3 (2001): 185–195; S.A. Cong and B.L. Low, "Treatment of Kleptomania with Fluvoxamine." *Acta Psychiatrica Scandinavia* 93 (1996): 314–315; J.E. Kraus, "Treatment of Kleptomania with Paroxetine," *Journal of Clinical Psychiatry* 60 (1999): 793

63. L.M. Koran, E.N. Aboujaoude, and N.N. Gamel. "Escitalopram Treatment of Kleptomania: An Open-Label Trial Followed by Double-Blind Discontinuation," *Journal of Clinical Psychiatry* 68 (2002): 422–427.

64. S. Kindler et al., "Emergency of Kleptomania During Treatment for Depression with Serotonin Selective Reuptake Inhibitors," *Clinical Neuropharmacology* 20/2 (1997): 126–129.

65. Grant, "Kleptomania," 175–201.

66. Ibid.

67. Marcus J. Goldman, "Kleptomania: Making Sense of the Nonsensical," *American Journal of Psychiatry* 148/8 (1991): 986–996.

68. Ibid.

69. Grant, "Kleptomania," 175–201.

70. Sherri MacKay et al., "Fire Interest and Antisociality as Risk Factors in the Severity and Persistence of Juvenile Firesetting," *Journal of the American Academy of Child Adolescent Psychiatry* 546/9 (2006) 1077–1084.

71. Ronald C. Kessler et al., "The Prevalence and Correlates of DSM-IV Intermittent Explosive Disorder in the National Comorbidity Survey Replication," *Archives of General Psychiatry* 63 (June 2006): 669–678.

72. Hermano Tavares, et al., "Factors at Play in Faster Progression for Female Pathological Gamblers: An Exploratory Analysis," *Journal of Clinical Psychiatry* 65/4 (April 2003): 433–438.

73. Elias Aboujaoude, Nona Gamel, and Lorrin M. Kora, "Overview of kleptomania and phenomenological description of 40 patients," *Primary Care Companion to the Journal of Clinical Psychiatry* 6/6 (2004): 244–247.

74. Kessler et al, "The Prevalence and Correlates of DSM-IV Intermittent Explosive Disorder in the National Comorbidity Survey Replication," 669–678.

75. David Tolin et al., "Pediatric Trichotillomania: Descriptive Psychopathology and an Open Trial

of Cognitive Behavioral Therapy," *Cognitive Behaviour Therapy* 36/3 (2007) :129–144.

76. Tavares et al., "Factors at Play in Faster Progression for Female Pathological Gamblers: An Exploratory Analysis," 433–438.

77. Michel Lejoyeux, et al., "Study of Impulse-Control Disorders among Alcohol-Dependent Patients," *Journal of Clinical Psychiatry* 60/5 (May 1999): 302–305.

78. Toneatto, Tony, "Relationship Between Gender and Substance Use Among Treatment-seeking Gamblers." *Gambling Research: The Electronic Journal of Gambling Issues.* June 23, 2002. Available online at http://www.camh.net/egambling/issue1/research. Accessed April 23, 2008.

79. Angela Ibáñez, Carlos Blanco, Paula Moreryra, and Jerónimo Sáiz-Ruiz, "Gender Differences in Pathological Gambling," *Journal of Clinical Psychiatry* 64/3 (March 2003): 295–301.

80. Tavares et al. "Factors at Play in Faster Progression for Female Pathological Gamblers: An Exploratory Analysis," 433–438.

81. Kessler et al., "The Prevalence and Correlates of DSM-IV Intermittent Explosive Disorder in the National Comorbidity Survey Replication," 669–678.

82. Aboujaoude, Gamel, and Koran, "Overview of Kleptomania and Phenomenological Description of 40 Patients," 244–247.

83. Kessler et al, "The Prevalence and Correlates of DSM-IV Intermittent Explosive Disorder in the National Comorbidity Survey Replication," 669–678.

84. American Psychiatric Association, *Diagnostic and Statistical Manual of Disorders. Fourth Edition, Text Revision. DSM-IV-TR.* (Washington, D.C: American Psychiatric Association, 2000), 100.

85. National Library of Medicine and the National Institutes of Health, "Oppositional Defiant Disorder," February 6, 2008. Available online at http://www.nlm.nih.gov/medlineplus/ency/article/001537.htm. Downloaded March 18, 2008.

86. National Library of Medicine and the National Institutes of Health, "Conduct Disorder," November 15, 2006. Available online at http://www.nlm.nih.gov/medlineplus/ency/article/000919.htm. Downloaded March 18, 2008.

87. American Psychiatric Association, Diagnostic and Statistical Manual of Disorders, 93.

88. National Institute of Mental Health, "Cold, Unfeeling Traits Linked to Distinctive Patterns in Kids with Severe Conduct Problems: Brain's Amygdala Region Less Responsive to Other People's Distress Signals," February 20, 2008. Available online at http://www.nimh.nih.gov/science-news/2008/cold-unfeeling-traits-linked-to-distinctive-brain-patterns-in-kids-with-severe-conduct-problems.shtml. Downloaded March 18, 2008.

89. Otto Kausch, "Suicide Attempts Among Veterans Seeking Treatment

for Pathological Gambling," *Journal of Clinical Psychiatry* 64/9 (September 2003): 1031–1038.

90. Ibáñez, Blanco, Moreryra, and Sáiz-Ruiz, "Gender Differences in Pathological Gambling," 295–301.

91. Nancy M. Petry, *Pathological Gambling: Etiology, Comorbidity, and Treatment.* Washington, D.C: American Psychological Association, 2005.

92. Bernardo Dell'Osso et al., "Epidemiologic and Clinical Updates on Impulse Control Disorders: A Critical Review," *European Archives of Psychiatry and Clinical Neuroscience* 256 (2006): 464–475.

93. Jon E. Grant, "Kleptomania," in *Clinical Manual of Impulse-Control Disorders*, eds. Eric Hollander, and Dan J. Stein (Washington, D.C.: American Psychiatric Publishing, 2006), 175–201.

94. Agnes van Minnen et al., "Treatment of Trichotillomania with Behavioral Therapy or Fluoxetine: A Randomized, Waiting-List Controlled Study," *Archives of General Psychiatry* 60 (May 2003): 517–522.

95. Giuseppe Hautmann, Jana Hercogova, and Torello Lotti, "Trichotillomania," *Journal of the American Academy of Dermatology* 46 (2002): 807–826.

96. David Tolin et al., "Pediatric Trichotillomania: Descriptive Psychopathology and an Open Trial of Cognitive Behavioral Therapy," *Cognitive Behaviour Therapy* 36/3 (2007) :129–144.

97. Stefano Pallanti, Nicolò Baldini Rossi, and Eric Hollander, "Pathological Gambling," in *Clinical Manual of Impulse Control Disorders*, eds. Eric Hollander and Dan J. Stein (Arlington, Va.: American Psychiatric Publishing, 2006), 251–289.

98. Ibid.

99. Emil F. Coccaro and Melany Danehy, "Intermittent Explosive Disorder," in *Clinical Manual of Impulse Control Disorders*, eds. Eric Hollander and Dan J. Stein (Arlington, Va.: American Psychiatric Publishing, 2006): 19–37.

100. Michel Lejoyeux, Mary McLoughlin, and Jean Adès, "Pyromania," in *Clinical Manual of Impulse Control Disorders*, eds. Eric Hollander and Dan J. Stein (Arlington, Va.: American Psychiatric Publishing, 2006), 229–250.

101. Jon E. Grant, Brian Odlaug, and Suck Won Kim, "Impulse Control Disorders: Clinical Characteristics and Pharmacological Management," *Psychiatric Times* 24/10 (September 2007). Available online at http://www.psychiatrictimes.com/display/article/10168/54046. Downloaded March 21, 2008.

102. Jon E. Grant and Suck Won Kim, "An Open-Label Study of Naltrexone in the Treatment of Kleptomania," *Journal of Clinical Psychiatry* 63/4 (April 2002): 349–356.

103. Pinhas N. Dannon, Iulian Iancu, and Leon Grunhaus, "Naltrexone Treatment in Kleptomaniac Patients," *Human Psychopharmacology: Clinical and Experimental* 14/8 (1999): 583–585.

104. Jon E. Grant, "Understanding and Treating Kleptomania: New Models

and New Treatments," *Israel Journal of Psychiatry and Related Sciences* 43/2 (2006): 81–87.

105. Jon E. Grant and Brian L. Odlaug, "Kleptomania: Clinical Characteristics and Treatment," *Revista Brasileira de Psiquiatria* (2008). Available online at http://www.scielo.br/scielo.php?script=sci_arttext&pid=S1516-44462006005000054&lng=en&nrm=iso&tlng=en. Downloaded March 21, 2008.

106. Bernardo Dell'Osso et al., "Epidemiologic and Clinical Updates on Impulse Control Disorders: A Critical Review," *European Archives of Psychiatry and Clinical Neuroscience* 256 (2006): 464–475.

107. Ibid.

108. William G. McCown and William A. Howatt, *Treating Gambling Problems.* New York: John Wiley & Sons, 2007.

109. R.L. O'Sullivan, G.A. Christenson, and D.J. Stein, "Pharmacotherapy of Trichotillomania," in *Trichotillomania*, eds. D.J. Stein, G.A. Christenson, and E. Hollander. (Washington,

D.C.: American Psychiatric Press, 1999), 93–124; Avinash De Sousa, "An Open-label Pilot Study of Naltrexone in Childhood-Onset Trichotillomania," *Journal of Child and Adolescent Psychopharmacology* 18/1 (2008): 30–33.

110. Jon E. Grant, "Letter to the Editor: SPECT Imaging and Treatment of Pyromania," *Journal of Clinical Psychiatry* 67/6 (June 2006): 998.

111. Dan J. Stein, Brian Harvey, Soraya Seedat, and Eric Hollander, "Treatment of Impulse-Control Disorders," in *Clinical Manual of Impulse-Control Disorders*, eds. Eric Hollander and Dan J. Stein (Arlington, Va.: American Psychiatric Press, 2006), 309–325.

112. National Institutes of Health, "Found 41 studies with search of "impulse control disorders". ClinicalTrials.gov. Available online at http://clinicaltrials.gov/ct2/results?cond=%22Impulse+Control+Disorders%22. Downloaded June 16, 2008.

GLOSSARY

antidepressants—Medications used to treat people with clinical depression as well as those with impulse disorders accompanied by depression. There are many types of antidepressants, and it is up to the psychiatrist to select the most appropriate medication for the disorder.

bipolar disorder—A psychiatric problem characterized by manic behavior that alternates with depressed behavior. If the individual has bipolar disorder in addition to an impulse control disorder, both conditions should be taken into account before any medication is prescribed.

cognitive-behavioral therapy (CBT)—A popular form of therapy for impulse control disorders and many other psychiatric disorders in which the individual is taught to challenge irrational thought processes and replace them with more logical thoughts.

comorbid—Existing simultaneously. In psychiatric terms, co-occurring with the main problem being studied. For example, depression or anxiety disorders may be comorbid with impulse control disorders.

conduct disorder—A psychiatric disorder characterized by lying, cheating, and stealing. It may be preceded by oppositional defiant disorder. Some individuals with impulse control disorders may also have conduct disorder.

domestic violence—Physical and/or emotional attacks on a family member such as a spouse, partner, or child.

firesetter—Another word for pyromaniac, or a person who impulsively starts fires for the thrill of it. The word *firestarter* is also sometimes used.

hair pulling—The act of pulling out one's hair; the behavior of a person with trichotillomania.

imaginal desensitization—A form of psychotherapy for individuals with kleptomania, who are instructed to imaging stealing an item while they are relaxed. They are then told to imagine the same scene while thinking about the many possible negative consequences that may occur with stealing.

impulse control disorder (ICD)—Disorder that is characterized by impulsivity or lack of control, and which causes distress to the individual.

Examples of impulse control disorders are pathological gambling, intermittent explosive disorder, kleptomania, pyromania, and trichotillomania.

kleptomania—An impulse control disorder that causes individuals to steal items that they do not need and that in many cases they could afford to purchase.

intermittent explosive disorder (IED)—An impulse control disorder that is characterized by unprovoked rage and physical attacks on other individuals and/or their property.

oppositional defiant disorder—A diagnosis in childhood or adolescence in which the individual refuses to follow the orders or requests of parents or other authority figures. Oppositional defiant disorder may develop into conduct disorder. Some impulse control disorders are associated with oppositional defiant disorder.

pathological gambling—An impulse control disorder that causes individuals to frequently gamble to the extent that it seriously impairs them at work and at home.

psychotherapy—A psychological means to treat a person with an impulse control disorder or other psychiatric problem. There are many different types of psychotherapy.

pyromania—An impulse control disorder characterized by the frequent impulsive need to set fires.

Rapunzel syndrome—A phrase used to describe the behavior of a person who pulls out and eats their hair.

road rage—Extremely aggressive behavior that is exhibited by a driver and which is out of proportion to real or imagined offenses committed by other drivers. The individual with road rage may follow the cars of those he feels have offended him (by cutting him off or performing other actions) and may physically assault them. The person with road rage may have intermittent explosive disorder.

selective serotonin reuptake inhibitors (SSRI)—A class of antidepressants that increases the blood levels of serotonin. These drugs may be effective in treating some impulse control disorders.

serotonin norepinephrine reuptake inhibitors—Antidepressant medications that increase the blood levels of both serotonin and norepinephrine.

trichobezoar—A human hairball that is found in the digestive system of a person who has pulled out and eaten their hair. (Hair is indigestible.) This can be a life-threatening condition.

trichophagia—The practice of pulling out and then eating one's own hair. This can be dangerous because human hair is indigestible and collects in the gastrointestinal tract.

trichotillomania—An impulse control disorder that causes an individual to extract a large quantity of the hair on the head and sometimes the hair on other parts of the body as well.

Books

Bayer, Linda. *Out of Control: Gambling and Other Impulse-Control Disorders.* Philadelphia: Chelsea House Publications, 2000.

Grant, Jon E. *Impulse Control Disorders: A Clinician's Guide to Understanding and Treating Behavioral Addictions.* New York: W.W. Norton, 2008.

Grant, Jon E., and Suck Won Kim. *Stop Me Because I Can't Stop Myself : Taking Control of Impulsive Behavior.* New York: McGraw-Hill, 2002.

Goldman, Marcus J., M.D. *Kleptomania: The Compulsion to Steal—What Can Be Done?* Far Hills, NJ: New Horizons Press, 1997.

Hollander, Eric, and Daniel J. Stein, eds. *Clinical Manual of Impulse Control Disorders.* Arlington, VA: American Psychiatric Publishing, 2006.

Libal, Autumn. *Drug Therapy and Impulse-Control Disorders.* Broomall, PA: Mason Crest Publishers, 2004.

McIntosh, Kenneth, and Phyllis Livingston. *Youth with Impulse Control Disorders: On the Spur of the Moment.* Philadelphia: Mason Crest Publishers, 2008.

Stein, Dan J., Gary Christenson, and Eric Hollander, eds. *Trichotillomania.* Washington, DC: American Psychiatric Publishing, 1999.

Web Sites

American Counseling Association

http://www.counseling.org

American Mental Health Counselors Association

http://www.amhca.org

American Pharmacists Association

http://www.pharmacists.com

American Psychiatric Association

http://www.psych.org

American Psychological Association

http://www.apa.org

Gamblers Anonymous

http://www.gamblersanonymous.org

Institute for Problem Gambling

http://gp.databytechknow.com

Mood and Anxiety Disorders Program, National Institute of Mental Health

http://intramural.nimh.nih.gov/mood

National Alliance on Mental Illness

http://www.nami.org

Mental Health America

http://www.nmha.org

National Mental Health Consumers' Self-Help Clearinghouse

http://www.mhselfhelp.org

Substance Abuse & Mental Health Services Administration

http://www.samhsa.gov

Trichotillomania Learning Center

http://www.trich.org

ABOUT THE AUTHOR

Christine Adamec is a medical writer who has authored and coauthored books on a broad array of topics, including diabetes, drug abuse, fibromyalgia, and prostate cancer. Her most recent books are *The Encyclopedia of Drug Abuse* and *The Encyclopedia of Elder Care* (both for Facts On File, 2008).